In short, daily readings from Scripture married to pointed, pithy comments and applications, Dean Merrill helps parents to see things from an eternal perspective and address parenting with a spiritual dimension. Very good and very helpful.

D. STUART BRISCOE *Elmbrook Church, Waukesha, Wisconsin*

Single parents and parents of blended families will find this devotional particularly helpful. Dean is sensitive to these situations and gives many biblical illustrations of single parents and blended families. He encourages these parents by reminding them that God can help them be good parents in these difficult situations.

ROGER MOREHEAD *David C. Cook Publishing Company*

How I wish this answer-filled book had been available when John and I were raising our family! In segments brief enough to fit into a parent's most hectic day, Dean Merrill presents a Bible passage (in everyday-English translation) and shows how that Scripture relates to the issues families face: sibling rivalry, over-stretched budgets, moving to a new town, high-pressure schedules, the dirty socks on the bedroom floor. Both Bible-centered and day-to-day practical.

ELIZABETH SHERRILL *author*

There's value everywhere here, though I've never before lauded a book for its appendix, but this has got to be a first! Believe me, Dean Merrill's *Wait Quietly* is valuable throughout, but the practical material just in those final few pages alone is worth the price of the book!

JACK W. HAYFORD *The Church on the Way, Van Nuys, California*

A remarkable book . . . a parents' preparation package! Just glancing at the title you would never believe this book is as powerful as it is. An insightful family manual based on actual family scenes from the Bible. It is like a journey through familiar territory where the old landscape has been greatly enhanced and the sign posts made much clearer. . . . A comfort and a catapult!

J. ALLAN PETERSEN *Family Concern*

I wish all the hurting people I see as a psychiatrist could have grown up in a home that had been guided by *Wait Quietly's* solid wisdom. Since they can't go back, at least they can have real help in not repeating the harmful patterns that busy parents so easily establish.

LOUIS MCBURNEY *Marble Retreat*

Dean Merrill helps us to do what is so difficult: Wait quietly before the Lord. These are devotions for parents—busy parents. . . . Whether a single parent, a stepparent, a foster parent—there is helpful material here for you in this devotional book, *Wait Quietly.*

ROGER C. PALMS *Decision magazine*

You'll find focus, priorities, strength and inspiration in the few moments you take each day with this book. . . . *Wait Quietly* provided some excellent discussion with my wife, and it daily reminded me that in the midst of a fast-paced lifestyle there is absolutely nothing more important for the family than being reminded of the precious gift God has given us in our children.

JIM BURNS *National Institute of Youth Ministry*

How refreshing to find a devotional book that focuses on marriage and family. . . . It is so nourishing that, as a couple, we started using it for our breakfast devotions before it was ever typeset.

JIM AND SALLY CONWAY *Mid-Life Dimensions*

Merrill's crisp writing style enables moms and dads to curl up with his book in less than five minutes for a daily biblical lesson on elevating their roles as parents to a higher and more godly level.

CASEY BANAS *Chicago Tribune*

When it is easy to lose sight of the high calling of parenting in the daily demands of survival, Dean Merrill lovingly invites us back to contemplate the real priorities behind parenting. Reading *Wait Quietly* is like sitting down at a quiet alpine lake and being reminded of what's truly significant—the love and nurture of our spouse and our children.

WAYNE JACOBSEN *The Savior's Community, Visalia, California*

A resource for every parent living at the breakneck pace of the nineties. He brings us back to listen to God, to each other, and to our inner selves. *Wait Quietly* offers a stimulating challenge to build our marriages and families in line with the mandates and promises of Scripture.

PAUL BORTHWICK *Grace Chapel, Lexington, Massachusetts*

Warm, wise counsel! Merrill carefully mines Scripture for a wealth of practical insights of vital and immediate use to us all.

HAROLD L. MYRA *Christianity Today*

This is not a book you simply enjoy reading once and then discard. This book should be kept *close-at-hand* as a life preserver when storms come against the home.

MIKE ADKINS *Mike Adkins Ministry*

Wait Quietly uses as its foundations the most perfect instruction book of all the Word of God. As a pediatrician in private practice for twenty-six years, I can appreciate the value of this book in encouraging, equipping, and motivating parents in their increasingly difficult roles.

J. THOMAS FITCH *San Antonio, Texas*

I commend Dean Merrill for his diligence in putting together a book of inspiration and instruction that will help us as parents in the busy world of today. Read it and be inspired!

WARREN HECKMAN *Lake City Church, Madison, Wisconsin*

A breath of fresh air for parents who feel overwhelmed and unprepared for the complex issues of parenting. What a great gift for all of us who need God's direction as mothers and fathers.

DALE HANSON BOURKE *author and mother*

Dean Merrill knows what happens at your place, and stretched-to-the-max parents can count on a friendly uplift from him. Leaving academic discussion of complex family theory to others, he gets down into the trenches and tackles such subjects as in-laws relationships, single parents, stepfathers and child favoritism. You will also want to read about such mundane but sensitive things as putdown humor, tiredness and griping.

LLOYD JACOBSEN *Bethel Christian Church, San Francisco, California*

Wait Quietly runs cross-grain to the hurried and harried lives parents live today. The prophet's indictment, In quietness and trust is your strength but you would have none of it, is more relevant to our culture than that of Isaiah's. May parents and grandparents take advantage of this excellent nurturing resource. It is a four-star devotional.

ROY C. PRICE *Monte Vista Chapel, Turlock, California*

WAIT QUIETLY

DEVOTIONS *for a* BUSY PARENT

DEAN MERRILL

TYNDALE HOUSE PUBLISHERS, INC.
WHEATON • ILLINOIS

CONTENTS

INTRODUCTION: MORE THAN A FEW ONE-LINERS

I f you're part of a household—especially one with children—you've no doubt gone hunting for good advice in print. In your quest to be a good spouse, to succeed as a mom or dad, you've scanned the newsstands and library racks. You've subscribed to parenting magazines. You've bought (or borrowed) books by the experts: T. Berry Brazelton, Benjamin Spock, Haim Ginott, James Dobson.

After all, keeping a family together is no small task. You've wanted all the help you could get.

Here's an odd question: *How about help from the Bible?*

Well, as most people know, the Bible doesn't say much *specifically about marriage and parenting*, does it? A few good lines like "Husbands, love your wives" . . . "Children, obey your parents" . . . "Train up a child in the way he should go" . . . "Thou shalt not commit adultery." But no in-depth seminars on the topic. There's no "First Epistle of Married Life" in the index. The Bible, it is assumed, has its head too far into the heavenlies to deal with household budgets and cranky spouses and obnoxious kids.

Wrong.

This book will show you the Bible in a fresh new light—a family light. Over the many months I have worked on this book, I have been amazed at how strongly the Bible connects with household issues once we begin to pay attention. Most of its insight is *not* in straight-on lecture form; it's in the stories of real-life husbands and wives, what they faced, the mistakes they made, the ways God rescued them if they were open to his input. The Scripture is, in fact, a wealth of family teaching.

This is not a book to read *with* your children, family-devotion style. This is "for adults only." It is intended to strengthen, encourage, and disciple *you*—the husband, wife, father, mother. If we adults learn to think biblically about the issues we face, to pattern our thoughts and actions after Scripture, the effect will be noticeable to those we live with.

Unlike most devotional books on the market today, I have insisted on printing the actual biblical text on these pages. That is because I believe that what the Bible has to say is central; it is not just a jumping-off point or a little historical prelude to what I want to say. It is, instead, "given to us by inspiration from God and is useful to teach us what is true and to make us realize what is wrong in our lives; it straightens us out and helps us do what is right" (2 Tim. 3:16).

So I have not gone through the Bible looking for proof texts, for clever one-liners to introduce the points *I* wanted to make. I have rather opened the Book and invited it to speak to me, as a husband of twenty-eight years and a father of three children, so that I might have something eternal to pass along to you. May God speak to you through these pages.

WAIT QUIETLY

My soul claims the Lord as my inheritance; therefore I will hope in him. The Lord is wonderfully good to those who wait for him, to those who seek for him. It is good both to hope and wait quietly for the salvation of the Lord. It is good for a young man to be under discipline, for it causes him to sit apart in silence beneath the Lord's demands. (Lam. 3:24-28)

So there is a full complete rest *still waiting* for the people of God. Christ has already entered there. He is resting from his work, just as God did after the creation. Let us do our best to go into that place of rest, too, being careful not to disobey God as the children of Israel did, thus failing to get in. (Heb. 4:9-11)

The late Corrie ten Boom, heroic survivor of Nazi death camps, was never a wife or mother—but she knew the truth when she wrote, "If the devil cannot make us bad, he will make us busy."

Have you noticed how hard it is, in the midst of family responsibilities, to *wait quietly* for the Lord . . . to *sit apart in silence* . . . to find time to *rest* and reflect on the meaning of your ceaseless activity?

Busy is in some ways a four-letter word. It is also a mandatory word; you *have* to say it. One modern mom meets another: "Hi—how have you been?" "Oh, really busy!" If you're *not* busy every day, all day long, what's the matter with you?

The above Scriptures do not call us to laziness. But they do call us to rest, to meditation, to quietness, to an experience of time-out. Only then can we hear the still, small voice of the Master. Only then can we get our orders for the day. Only then can we center down, as the old Quakers used to say, and focus on eternal perspectives.

The life of a Christian husband or wife was not meant to equal frenzy and burnout. It is perfectly right to stop—to cease working, doing, accomplishing—in order to simply *be* God's child for a block of time.

This may go against our grain, our habit of tackling the jobs that cry for our attention. The King James Version renders Hebrews 4:11 as follows: "Let us labour therefore to enter into that rest." *Labour* to rest? Yes. We actually have to *work* at it. We have to force ourselves to sit down, to breathe deeply, to listen. But when we do, God empowers us to rise up and accomplish great things for him.

Lord . . . I'm here, and I'm quiet.
You are more important than all the

others who call for me to get busy.
What would you like to say to me today?

DOING THE WORD

Plan how to make this time a regular part of your days. When will you quiet yourself before the Lord? Where will you do it? Go to your personal calendar and write it down. Commit your plan to writing, and then follow through.

ON THE EDGE

Let us acknowledge the Lord;
let us press on to acknowledge him. (Hos. 6:3, NIV)

Trust in the Lord with all your heart
and lean not on your own understanding;
in all your ways acknowledge him,
and he will make your paths straight.
  The Lord's curse is on the house of the wicked,
but he blesses the home of the righteous.
(Prov. 3:5-6, 33, NIV)

When you think about holding a marriage together for sixty years, through good times and bad, and wonder what it really takes . . .

Or when you boil down the whole gargantuan project of raising children to its core, looking for the one secret of success, the key that allows you to turn out a respectable young adult instead of a serial killer . . .

It's not just common sense.

It's not just following the traditions of your parents and grandparents.

It's not luck.

It's not reading all the worthy advice of experts.

It is, rather, to "trust in the Lord" (Prov. 3:5).

That familiar Scripture does not rule out the usefulness of human understanding. Go ahead and read all the books, it seems to say. Talk to older, wiser generations about what they did right. Gather all the advice you can. *But don't lean on it.* It's not strong enough to carry you the distance.

Imagine that you're standing on the South Rim of the Grand Canyon, viewing the chasm below. There's a fence at the edge of the precipice, and various signs that tell you to be careful. Good advice. But don't go *leaning* on the fence or the signs. They might not be as sturdy as they look. Keep your weight firmly planted on the rock beneath your feet.

So it is with dodging the many pitfalls of family life. Human signs and warnings have their place, but the only real safety is to remain anchored to the Rock.

The familiar verse 6 does not say, "In all your *words* acknowledge him." Lip service to God is easy. Religious talk about the Lord is cheap. This verse calls us to give God his proper place in all our *ways:* our strategies, our planning, our habits, our responses to people, our projects.

The book of 2 Chronicles tells about a gifted king named Asa who won one battle against overwhelming odds by calling on the Lord, then turned around the next time and hired a foreign army to help him. "Because you *relied* on the king of Aram and not on the Lord your God," a prophet scolded him, "the army of the king of Aram has escaped from your hand. Were not the Cushites and Libyans a mighty army with great numbers of chariots and horsemen? Yet when you *relied* on the Lord, he delivered them into your hand" (2 Chron. 16:7-8, NIV, emphasis added).

The king didn't get the point; in fact, he got mad and threw the prophet in jail. Later in life, Asa was still missing it. An attack of something like gout struck him, and "though his disease was severe, even in his illness he did not seek help from the Lord, but only from the physicians" (16:12, NIV). Soon after, he died.

In the challenges you face this week, on what are you leaning?

———————

Lord, I really am not smart enough to keep my marriage perpetually alive and vibrant. I don't know enough to finish raising these children by myself. As the old hymn says, "I need thee—O I need thee; every hour I need thee." I want you to be the Rock beneath my feet; you are absolutely crucial to my success.

REINFORCING THE WORD

Get out a hymnal and read all the stanzas of "I Need Thee Every Hour." Sing or hum the song as a prayer to the Lord.

WHAT "I LOVE YOU" REALLY MEANS

Dear friends, let us practice loving each other, for love comes from God and those who are loving and kind show that they are the children of God, and that they are getting to know him better. But if a person isn't loving and kind, it shows that he doesn't know God—for God is love.

God showed how much he loved us by sending his only Son into this wicked world to bring to us eternal life through his death. In this act we see what real love is: it is not our love for God but his love for us when he sent his Son to satisfy God's anger against our sins.

Dear friends, since God loved us as much as that, we surely ought to love each other too. (1 John 4:7-11)

Quick—what one word in the English language is the opposite of *love?*

Hate?

War?

Violence?

There is a more stark antonym than any of these. It is far more widespread than slander or artillery. It is this: *apathy*. The attitude that says, "I don't care—do what you want—I'll take care of my life, and you take care of yours."

In the above text, how did God show that he loved? He *got involved*. He sent his Son into a messy world. And the apostle John says that if we claim to love a spouse, a child, or anyone else, we will get involved, too. We will do what God did.

That is much tougher than simply backing away. When a son or daughter whom we say we love turns stubborn, or chooses the wrong activity, or strays toward sloppiness, it is hard to act. After all, we don't want to cause a big fuss. How much easier to tell ourselves, "Oh well . . . he's just going through a stage. . . . Maybe I've misunderstood the facts. . . . I'm tired tonight, anyway."

In her classic little book *"If,"* Amy Carmichael wrote: "If I am afraid to speak the truth, lest I lose affection, or lest the one concerned should say, 'You do not understand,' or because I fear to lose my reputation for kindness; if I put my own good name before the other's highest good, then I know nothing of Calvary love."

Loving correction is part of love. But there is another side as well. The same principle of involvement is true when a family member does something *positive* and a warm affirmation is in order. The loving person says, "You were fantastic! I'm so proud of you." The apathetic person gives a faint smile and turns back to the TV program.

What is the proof of love? Involvement in the other person's life, engagement with what's *really* going on inside his or her mind and heart, caring enough to take the other person seriously. That's what God did with us. That's how we show that his love has invaded us.

———————

Lord, I confess there are times I'd just like to blot out my family members. I like being self-centered once in a while! Teach me to love like you love. Nudge me out of my apathy to extend myself with joy to those closest to me.

DOING THE WORD

Find a new way, in the next twenty-four hours, to *be* loving to each person in your family, *without* using the words *I love you*. Convey the essence of the phrase through your action instead.

King Rehoboam reigned seventeen years in Jerusalem. . . . But he was an evil king, for he never did decide really to please the Lord. (2 Chron. 12:13-14)

Since many of the people arriving . . . were ceremonially impure because they had not undergone the purification rites, . . . King Hezekiah prayed for them, and they were permitted to eat the Passover anyway, even though this was contrary to God's rules. But Hezekiah said, "May the good Lord pardon everyone who determines to follow the Lord God of his fathers, even though he is not properly sanctified for the ceremony." And the Lord listened to Hezekiah's prayer and did not destroy them. (2 Chron. 30:17-20)

[Ezra] asked to be allowed to return to Jerusalem, and the king granted his request; for the Lord his God was blessing him. Many ordinary people as well . . . traveled with him. . . . The Lord gave them a good trip. This was because Ezra had determined to study and obey the laws of the Lord and to become a Bible teacher, teaching those laws to the people of Israel. (Ezra 7:6-10)

Wouldn't you feel awful to have Rehoboam's epitaph engraved on *your* tombstone? To have your life summed up by the statement, "This person, in spite of starting out with great advantages, turned out to be a flop, because he never could quite make up his mind to please the Lord"? What a tragedy.

By contrast, Ezra got high marks for his allegiance to God. And the visitors to Hezekiah's Passover festival even got to skip a few of the minor Old Testament regulations because in their hearts they had determined to follow the Lord. The key difference in these accounts revolves around the verbs *decide and determine.*

Have you *decided* whom to serve? Have you *determined*—made up your mind—to let God call the shots? Have you then notified your heart, your emotions, that he is Lord; i.e., Boss, Authority, the One in Charge?

Have you notified your spouse and children of these decisions, not only in words but by your actions? As they watch your consistency in prayer and in absorbing the Scripture, or your approach to life's multitude of choices, what would they say about your allegiance?

Popular music today says the heart is uncontrollable, a Mexican jumping bean that does whatever it will, hopping from one loyalty to another without much notice. If the mood shifts, what can you do but just go with the flow?

God's Word says we *can* control our emotions. We can order them to cling to the Lord wholeheartedly. And when

11

we settle that loyalty, he proceeds to bless us—as well as those with whom we live.

_____

Lord, in the words of the simple chorus from India, I have decided to follow you—no turning back, no turning back.

REINFORCING THE WORD

Write this Scripture on a card and stick it on the mirror in your bathroom or bedroom: *Your statutes are my heritage forever; they are the joy of my heart. My heart is set on keeping your decrees to the very end. (Ps. 119:111-112, NIV)*

R.H.I.P.

Don't be selfish; don't live to make a good
impression on others. Be humble, thinking of others as
better than yourself. Don't just think about your own affairs, but be interested in others, too, and in what they
are doing.

Your attitude should be the kind that was shown us by
Jesus Christ, who, though he was God, did not demand
and cling to his rights as God, but laid aside his mighty
power and glory, taking the disguise of a slave and becoming like men. And he humbled himself even further,
going so far as actually to die a criminal's death on a
cross.

Yet it was because of this that God raised him up to
the heights of heaven and gave him a name which is
above every other name, that at the name of Jesus every
knee shall bow in heaven and on earth and under the
earth, and every tongue shall confess that Jesus Christ is
Lord, to the glory of God the Father. (Phil. 2:3-11)

There's a saying in the military: "R.H.I.P.—Rank Has Its Privileges." In other words, colonels get to do things that captains only dream of. And colonels *get out of doing* things that enlisted men have to endure.

Jesus, however, did not strut like a colonel. His kingdom was not organized by rank and pecking order. Although he held the special commission of Son of God, Savior of the world, he felt no need to remind people of it.

Verse 6 is a powerful countermand to us assertive, contentious, honor-seeking types: "Though he was God, [Jesus] did not demand and cling to his rights." Jesus had every *right* to demand respect, wealth, and pampering—but he seemed not to care. If the Pharisees didn't show him proper deference, so what? If the scribes belittled his teachings, he merely shrugged. He had nothing to prove.

In fact, he was content to live with a secret—his divinity. He covered it up with "the disguise of a slave" (v. 7) as he focused attention and energy on other people. Yet he went down in history as the Greatest of the great.

Fathers and mothers who demand to be respected, who flaunt their status, who lecture about the line of authority usually evoke nothing but sullenness. Husbands who insist on special privileges find themselves alone and resented. Wives who manipulate to get compliments and attention most often fail to receive what they crave.

Why? Because their focus is on themselves rather than others. The family members around them can smell the self-serving agenda. It is amazing to notice that as Jesus humbled himself in the eyes of creatures far less important than he, "God raised him up to the heights" (v. 9). God bestowed upon him a rank with which no one could argue. Such is the reward of the willing servant—in the world, in the church, and yes, in the home.

It sounds upside-down, and it is. It goes against the modern notion of looking out for number one. "But among you it is quite different," Jesus told his disciples. "Anyone wanting to be a leader among you must be your servant. And if you want to be right at the top, you must serve like a slave. Your attitude must be like my own, for I, the Messiah, did not come to be served, but to serve, and to give my life as a ransom for many" (Matt. 20:26-28).

Lord, help me to relax in your approval alone.
Show me what my household truly needs, and
then help me to be willing to provide it, even if
the act is not very prestigious for me.
Strike my pride and make me more like Jesus,
the humble servant of all.

DOING THE WORD

Choose two mundane chores around your house and take care of them anonymously, without drawing anyone's attention to your deeds.

A Castle Called "We"

Wives, fit in with your husbands' plans. . . .
Don't be concerned about the outward beauty that depends on jewelry, or beautiful clothes, or hair arrangement. Be beautiful inside, in your hearts, with the lasting
charm of a gentle and quiet spirit that is so precious to
God.

You husbands must be careful of your wives, being
thoughtful of their needs and honoring them as the
weaker sex. Remember that you and your wife are partners in receiving God's blessings, and if you don't treat
her as you should, your prayers will not get ready answers. (1 Pet. 3:1, 3-4, 7)

There's enough in this short passage to make everybody
squirm. It challenges our cherished images of being
independent, self-assured, unencumbered, captains of our
own fate.

What the apostle has in mind is marriage as an invisible

province, a commonwealth of two minds and wills ready to bend and flex for one another. The phrase "partners in receiving God's blessings" (v. 7) is translated in the Revised Standard Version "joint heirs of the grace of life." What does that mean? It means procreation, for one thing: New life is born only from the joining of male and female. And therein lies a model for a thousand other endeavors in marriage. When husband and wife blend their unique efforts in willing cooperation with each other, wondrous results occur.

Just as a husband and wife are a single unit in financial matters, so they are to God. The mortgage company and the Internal Revenue Service think of us as John *and* Susan Smith, facing all liabilities together. God sees us as inseparable partners awaiting his blessing.

We are like a medieval castle with one bold flagstaff. Prior to the wedding, our individual pennants used to read "Me." But now the initial letter has been turned upside-down, so that it reads "We." *We* are a unit. *We* are a team. *We* look out for each other. *We* are joint (and joined) heirs.

Ambrose Bierce, a turn-of-the-century journalist, had it right when he wrote, "Marriage is a community consisting of a master, a mistress, and two slaves, making in all, two." That kind of community, says the apostle, is able to raise prayers that get God's attention. Religious people have posed a dozen different reasons for unanswered prayer, but this one—the lack of marital harmony and considerateness—is often conveniently skipped.

Peter, the only apostle clearly identified in the New Testament as married (Mark 1:29-31), was on to something here.

The closer we draw to one another, the closer we are allowed to God's throne.

_____

Lord, yielding to you is somehow easier than
yielding to my spouse. Help me to do both, so
that you can bless our union.

REMEMBERING THE WORD

Since this is one of the Bible's few passages that gives straight-on advice to spouses, memorize the section that applies to you:

Husbands: 1 Peter 3:7
Wives: 1 Peter 3:1-4

BE DIRECT

The Lord appeared to Abraham near the
great trees of Mamre while he was sitting at the entrance
to his tent in the heat of the day. Abraham looked up
and saw three men standing nearby. When he saw them,
he hurried from the entrance of his tent to meet them
and bowed low to the ground. He said, "If I have found
favor in your eyes, my lord, do not pass your servant by.
Let a little water be brought, and then you may all wash
your feet and rest under this tree."

When the men got up to leave, they looked down toward
Sodom, and Abraham walked along with them to see them
on their way. Then the Lord said, "Shall I hide from Abraham what I am about to do? Abraham will surely become
a great and powerful nation, and all nations on earth will
be blessed through him. For I have chosen him, so that he
will direct his children and his household after him to
keep the way of the Lord by doing what is right and just,
so that the Lord will bring about for Abraham what he has
promised him." (Gen. 18:1-4, 16-19, NIV)

Whatever you do, modern parent, be sure not to force religion down your children's throats. Let them make up their own minds—or so say the pop experts of our time.

The divine Visitor who stopped to see Abraham long ago apparently didn't subscribe to such a philosophy. Not that he coerced the young (or old) to serve him whether they liked it or not; after all, the whole notion of giving people a free choice was his to begin with.

But that didn't hinder him from commissioning parents, especially fathers, to "direct" their children and households "to keep the way of the Lord." He fully expected Abraham to take leadership in his home regarding spiritual matters, to set a pace, to let his offspring know that "doing what is right and just" was expected procedure.

There is no way to read this without seeing a proactive role for Abraham.

Such a man, said the Lord, was a person to be trusted with divine secrets (v. 17). Such a man was also a person whom God would bless with fulfilled promises (vv. 18-19). Once Abraham had proven faithful and reliable on the household level, God could well afford to honor him in more public arenas.

Just as we train our children to value their country, their grandparents, or their school, we can also train them to love God. We need not hesitate. It's part of our assignment.

Lord, you know I have decided to follow you
with my whole heart. Give me courage and
wisdom to help my children do the same.

DOING THE WORD

In everyday conversation with family members, take care to position yourselves as "a *Christian* family," "a *Christian* home." When questions arise, respond with such things as "What do you think the Lord would want us to do?" Establish a definite identity as a household under the command of God himself.

TIRED?

A man will always reap just the kind of crop he
sows! If he sows to please his own wrong desires, he will
be planting seeds of evil and he will surely reap a harvest
of spiritual decay and death; but if he plants the good
things of the Spirit, he will reap the everlasting life that the
Holy Spirit gives him. And let us not get tired of doing
what is right, for after a while we will reap a harvest of
blessing if we don't get discouraged and give up. That's
why whenever we can we should always be kind to everyone, and especially to our Christian brothers. (Gal. 6:7-10)

When you're switching Laundry Load No. 6 into the dryer
and there are two loads yet to wash . . . when you write
the check for your child's music lessons and *again* there's
nothing left for an adult night out . . . when you play an
after-supper game with your kids, then read them a bedtime
story, pray with them, and finally tuck them in, only to realize
you're too tired to tackle that job you'd saved for this evening

. . . you need the apostle's exhortation in verse 9: "Let us not get tired of doing what is right, for after a while we will reap a harvest of blessing if we don't get discouraged and give up."

Parenting is like farming: a lot of hard work, day in and day out, month in and month out, and the "harvest of blessing" doesn't come quickly. It takes a special kind of perspective to raise kids.

Having kids is the easy part: a nine-month incubation that climaxes in the thrill of a new arrival. *Raising* kids, by comparison, takes twenty-five times as long and probably a hundred times as much endurance and fortitude. Lots of parents bail out early—not officially, of course, but practically. Somewhere along about junior high, they quit trying, quit pouring their energy and creativity into the process, start coasting, just hoping their offspring don't do anything *really bad* in the remaining months or years of their liability.

This Scripture, by contrast, says that "if we don't get discouraged and give up," the Holy Spirit will smile on us, and we will be able to finish our task with pride.

Lord, I give you my best effort today—whether my children realize it or not. Help me keep planting good seeds, and bless the harvest.

REINFORCING THE WORD

Memorize Galatians 6:9. It's one of the best Scriptures for the tough times of family life. *Let us not get tired of doing what is right, for after a while we will reap a harvest of blessing if we don't get discouraged and give up.*

CRUNCH TIME FOR A SINGLE MOM

One day the wife of one of the seminary students came to Elisha to tell him of her husband's death. He was a man who had loved God, she said. But he had owed some money when he died, and now the creditor was demanding it back. If she didn't pay, he said he would take her two sons as his slaves.

"What shall I do?" Elisha asked. "How much food do you have in the house?"

"Nothing at all, except a jar of olive oil," she replied.

"Then borrow many pots and pans from your friends and neighbors!" he instructed. "Go into your house with your sons and shut the door behind you. Then pour olive oil from your jar into the pots and pans, setting them aside as they are filled!"

So she did. Her sons brought the pots and pans to her, and she filled one after another! Soon every container was full to the brim!

"Bring me another jar," she said to her sons.

"There aren't any more!" they told her. And then the oil stopped flowing!

When she told the prophet what had happened, he said to her, "Go and sell the oil and pay your debt, and there will be enough money left for you and your sons to live on!" (2 Kings 4:1-7)

Does God notice the struggles of single parents? Yes— and he provides relief, although not always as quickly as we might wish.

This woman's breadwinner was gone, and he hadn't left any life insurance. Worse than that, he *had* left a stack of bills. The grace periods had all run out, and creditors were banging on the door.

She had nothing left to pawn. No real estate, no animals, no jewelry, nothing. Nothing, that is, except two wide-eyed little boys, who in that ruthless economy were fair game as legal tender.

She swallowed hard and then revealed her need to a trusted outsider. He asked a rather irrelevant-sounding question (v. 2), "How much food do you have in the house?" (A very similar question, by the way, to the one God asked another person who was stuck—Moses, at the burning bush: "What do you have there in your hand?" [Exod. 4:2].)

While we want God to swoop down from the sky and rescue us, he seems to like starting with resources near at hand.

So the prophet gave the mother an action plan that sounded odd at first. Should she trust this fellow? Was this just another piece of bogus advice, another dead end, a setup for another disappointment?

She elected to follow through. And only then did the miracle of God's provision show itself. God supplied—and her sons, fatherless and feeling forgotten, got to watch the whole thing. Her family would not disintegrate after all. The woman and her children could not help marveling at the Lord's last-minute rescue, pulling a single-parent family back from the brink. They wound up not only debt-free but with extra cash on hand for the future!

God is never late, but neither does he seem to be particularly early. He waits until we know we need his help, and then he opens his generous hand.

Lord, provide for my family today—your way.
Show me the part I must play, and take care of
the rest.

DOING THE WORD

- If you're a single parent, go ahead and ask God for a genuine miracle. Don't just assume you're stuck, trapped, boxed in; take a wild leap of faith and see what God might do.
- If you have a spouse, talk together about the single parents you know. Pick out one and think up a surprise to make his or her life a little easier.

FAITH THAT STICKS

Paul and Silas went first to Derbe and then on to Lystra where they met Timothy, a believer whose mother was a Christian Jewess, but his father a Greek. Timothy was well thought of by the brothers in Lystra and Iconium, so Paul asked him to join them on their journey. (Acts 16:1-3)

How I thank God for you, Timothy. . . . I know how much you trust the Lord, just as your mother Eunice and your grandmother Lois do; and I feel sure you are still trusting him as much as ever.

But you must keep on believing the things you have been taught. You know they are true, for you know that you can trust those of us who have taught you. You know how, when you were a small child, you were taught the holy Scriptures; and it is these that make you wise to accept God's salvation by trusting in Christ Jesus. (2 Tim. 1:3, 5; 3:14-15)

The rebel walks a thorny, treacherous road; the man who values his soul will stay away.

> Teach a child to choose the right path, and when he is older, he will remain upon it. (Prov. 22:5-6)

What was it that Eunice did right? How did she manage to raise a son whom the apostle Paul would later applaud as the best of his associates (see Phil. 2:20)?

Hers was not a "perfect Christian home." Eunice apparently got little help from her Gentile husband. She did get help and encouragement from her mother, Lois. Together they made an impression on a young boy, teaching him to love and revere the Bible, guiding him to put his trust in its Author.

Why did Timothy turn out like his mother and grandmother instead of like his father or his pagan peers in Lystra? He was taught, in the wonderful words of Proverbs 22:6, to "*choose* the right path," to select it for himself. He said yes to God's way and no to the other options.

The key verb is *choose*. A child will not stay on a path onto which he has been *forced*. Many a Christian parent has recited this Scripture (usually from the somewhat cloudy King James Version: "Train up a child in the way he should go . . .") and tried to claim it as a guarantee. The tone, if not the actual wording, has been, "Lord, for years I dragged that kid along the way he was supposed to go—now why has he departed from it?"

The verse is less an ironclad promise than it is a *proverb*—a statement of how things normally turn out. And a very big factor in seeing sons and daughters remain on the godly path is to carefully, gently bring them to the point of *personally choosing* it. Those who do not select it of their own volition will stray in time, and parents need not beat themselves over the head for their grown children's choices. But once a young person owns his faith in God for himself, not just for the sake of family tradition, he is much more likely to be a Christian for life.

Apparently that is what Eunice achieved with her son, Timothy. After all, she eventually came to the day when he left town with Paul and Silas—then what? She could no longer influence him. We know from reading the New Testament that he kept following the Lord, even to the point of going to prison for his faith (see Heb. 13:23).

May we raise up more of his kind.

Lord, more than anything else in my life I want to pass the torch of genuine faith to my children. Help me be bold to speak when I should, but not so bold that I short-circuit their decision-making process. May they freely, eagerly choose to love and serve you all the days of their life.

REFLECTING ON THE WORD

Think of an area in which you have been requiring your child to do the Christian thing: church attendance, perhaps, or personal devotions, or refusing questionable entertainment. Depending upon the age of your child, this action may be entirely appropriate! But since your goal is *self*-motivation and *self*-discipline, how will your son or daughter make this gradual shift? Are there ways you can begin now to cultivate more choosing on the child's part?

PATRIARCH WITH A PASSION

When Enoch had lived 65 years, he became the father of Methuselah. And after he became the father of Methuselah, Enoch walked with God 300 years and had other sons and daughters. Altogether, Enoch lived 365 years. Enoch walked with God; then he was no more, because God took him away. (Gen. 5:21-24, NIV)

By faith Enoch was taken from this life, so that he did not experience death; he could not be found, because God had taken him away. For before he was taken, he was commended as one who pleased God. (Heb. 11:5, NIV)

Notice the chronology. As long as Enoch was a regular young adult and new husband, nothing particular is said about him, either good or bad.

But as soon as he became a dad, something changed on the inside. His spiritual desire came alive. Perhaps the need to be a good role model hit him. Looking down at baby Methuselah in his arms, he couldn't help thinking, *I've got to get serious about my responsibility here. A new generation is starting up. How will this boy know right from wrong? How will he find his place in the world? I must show the way.*

This sudden awakening is perennial. Demographers tell us today that young adults, after a season of indifference, often come back to the church when their children arrive. They themselves may not have been in Sunday school for fifteen years, but they want their kids there. Spiritual moorings become important once again.

In Enoch's case, his sense of devotion stuck. Long after Methuselah and his siblings were out on their own, their father was still following God with all his heart. People commented about it, according to Hebrews; they said things like "Enoch sure tries to please the Lord, doesn't he?" It became a mark of his personality.

Finally, God decided this dad was ready for heaven ahead of time. He didn't need to finish a normal lifespan; he could come right away. One day, Enoch was suddenly missing. He had gone on to be with his Best Friend.

Is parenting drawing you closer to God? Are your children noticing that you and he just sort of seem to track together? Do the neighbors sense your complete reliance upon God for the day-to-day wisdom that child-raising demands? Are you driven to your knees for answers and solutions?

Walking with God is not just for saints and clergy. It is for ordinary fathers and mothers who know they cannot raise well-adjusted children alone.

O Lord, my deep desire is to match strides with you, to go where you go, to track alongside you—and talk with you all the while. Only you know how to raise these kids correctly. All the helpful books, classes, and videos in the world fall short. I need you. Let me, like Enoch, stay by your side always.

REFLECTING ON THE WORD

Ask yourself a scary question: *If I died right now, here in the middle of my years, what would people say about my walk with God? What would be my spiritual reputation? At my funeral, would the subject even come up?!* Then reflect on what you might do in your remaining years to be "commended as one who pleased God."

DANCING WITH DOLLARS

Do you want to be truly rich? You already are if you are happy and good. After all, we didn't bring any money with us when we came into the world, and we can't carry away a single penny when we die. So we should be well satisfied without money if we have enough food and clothing. But people who long to be rich soon begin to do all kinds of wrong things to get money, things that hurt them and make them evil-minded and finally send them to hell itself. For the love of money is the first step toward all kinds of sin. Some people have even turned away from God because of their love for it, and as a result have pierced themselves with many sorrows.

O Timothy, you are God's man. Run from all these evil things, and work instead at what is right and good, learning to trust him and love others and to be patient and gentle. (1 Tim. 6:6-11)

N otice the *emotional* words in this passage:
    "Do you *want* to be truly rich?"
"People who *long* to be rich . . ."

"For the *love* of money is the first step toward all kinds of sin. Some people have . . . pierced themselves *with many sorrows.*"

Dollars—silent pieces of metal and paper, with no life or personality of their own—have a peculiar way of getting our blood to race. We get excited about money. The mere thought of a bonus at work, a tax refund, a lucky lottery hit, or a surprise inheritance from Uncle Leonard sends our heart rate sprinting. *Wow, I can see it now—that new big-screen TV I've been wanting, a getaway weekend, new bikes for the kids . . . maybe we could even trade for a new minivan. . . .*

This is a bad pattern, says the apostle Paul. The problem with getting emotional about money is that every *up* carries with it the possibility (if not the probability) of a *down*. Every time we get elated about having extra money, we set ourselves up to get depressed as soon as we don't.

In verse 7, Paul points out that we all started life with a zero balance. As very small children, we had no money to call our own. (And do you remember how happy we were?) The line on our chart of financial assets is now traversing up and down, cresting and falling, rising again, then leveling out—but in the end, says Paul, we will come to a zero balance once again. We will die, someone will write checks out of our account to pay the funeral director, the cemetery, the federal tax authority, our various heirs—and the last line in the checkbook will again read $00.00.

So why get excited in the interim?

Instead, verse 11 lists goals that are truly worth our adrenaline: doing what is right and good, learning to trust God, loving other people, being patient and gentle. *These* are the pursuits that result in eternal treasure. These are the gains that make our heavenly Father go, "Yes!" Money comes, money goes. Character and godliness endure.

————————

*Lord, I want to do a better job of controlling
my attitude about money. When I get too
excited about having it—or depressed about not
having it—remind me to settle down.
Don't let me stray into the tragedies that
beset money lovers. I resolve to focus instead
on the qualities that you value.*

REINFORCING THE WORD

Memorize as much of the above passage as you can, to set a watchword within your mind. Even one verse will prove valuable in curbing "financial manic-depressive syndrome." The more verses the better.

THE STEPFATHER WHO CARED

These are the facts concerning the birth of Jesus Christ: His mother, Mary, was engaged to be married to Joseph. But while she was still a virgin she became pregnant by the Holy Spirit. Then Joseph, her fiancé, being a man of stern principle, decided to break the engagement but to do it quietly, as he didn't want to publicly disgrace her.

As he lay awake considering this, he fell into a dream, and saw an angel standing beside him. "Joseph, son of David," the angel said, "don't hesitate to take Mary as your wife! For the child within her has been conceived by the Holy Spirit. And she will have a Son, and you shall name him Jesus (meaning 'Savior'), for he will save his people from their sins. This will fulfill God's message through his prophets—

'Listen! The virgin shall conceive a child! She shall give birth to a Son, and he shall be called "Emmanuel" (meaning "God is with us").'"

When Joseph awoke, he did as the angel commanded
and brought Mary home to be his wife, but she remained a virgin until her Son was born; and Joseph
named him "Jesus."

After [the wise men] were gone, an angel of the Lord
appeared to Joseph in a dream. "Get up and flee to
Egypt with the baby and his mother," the angel said,
"and stay there until I tell you to return, for King Herod
is going to try to kill the child." That same night he left
for Egypt with Mary and the baby, and stayed there until
King Herod's death.

When Herod died, an angel of the Lord appeared in a
dream to Joseph in Egypt and told him, "Get up and
take the baby and his mother back to Israel, for those
who were trying to kill the child are dead."

So he returned immediately to Israel with Jesus and
his mother. But on the way he was frightened to learn
that the new king was Herod's son, Archelaus. Then, in
another dream, he was warned not to go to Judea, so
they went to Galilee instead and lived in Nazareth.
(Matt. 1:18-25; 2:13-15, 19-23)

The Bible doesn't call Joseph a stepdad, but that is exactly
what he was: the husband of a woman whose child was
not his own.

Yet that didn't stop him from playing a wise and benefi-
cient role in the family. He got involved. He stayed close to
God, so close that God spoke to him at least four times about
what the family should do.

One might have excused Joseph for holding back, acting

aloof, folding his arms as if to say, *This pregnancy is Mary's deal; I had nothing to do with it. Don't look to me; I'm a casual bystander. . . .* And after the birth: *The boy is hers, not mine. She'll have to take the lead on whatever he needs.*

But his response was quite the opposite. Look at Joseph's prominence in the Nativity story:

1. God directly tells *him* to proceed with the marriage (1:20).
2. He obeys (1:24).
3. He puts his natural sexual desire for his new bride on hold *for seven or eight months,* not wanting to interfere with whatever the Holy Spirit has started within Mary's body (1:25).
4. He names the baby as instructed (1:25).
5. Two years later, God tells him to emigrate—quickly (2:13).
6. Within a matter of *hours,* he's on the road (2:14).
7. When it's safe to return to his homeland, God gives Joseph a third message: Go back to Israel (2:20).
8. He immediately obeys (2:21).
9. On the way, God fine-tunes his destination (2:22).
10. Again, he leads his family as told (2:23).

The point of this story is that every kind of family— whether conventional, blended, reconstituted, or even highly unusual such as the holy family—can benefit from a strong, godly dad. Families are no different from companies, churches, or nations: they all need leadership, someone in touch with the mind of God, and willing to take action.

Granted, not every family has a Joseph, and many women

do an admirable job of guiding the household instead. But those of us men who love our spouse and the children within our care would do well to imitate the character and spiritual sensitivity of Jesus' stepfather.

Lord, teach me how my home might function better. Speak to me about things I should do, moves I should make for the benefit of everyone. Show me more about my particular role in the family structure. I want to hear your voice.

REFLECTING ON THE WORD

If you're a husband, think about whether you view yourself as a *leader*. Not just a wage earner, a car maintainer, a plumbing fixer . . . but a *leader* of your household. A person who plans ahead, who looks out for the general interest of the group, who encourages, who gives structure, who prays regularly about how the family is going. Does the word fit you?

SMART MOUTH

A fool is quick-tempered; a wise man stays cool when insulted.

When a man is trying to please God, God makes even his worst enemies to be at peace with him.

A wise man restrains his anger and overlooks insults. This is to his credit. (Prov. 12:16; 16:7; 19:11)

As David and his party passed Bahurim, a man came out of the village cursing them. It was Shimei, the son of Gera, a member of Saul's family. He threw stones at the king and the king's officers and all the mighty warriors who surrounded them!

"Get out of here, you murderer, you scoundrel!" he shouted at David. "The Lord is paying you back for murdering King Saul and his family; you stole his throne and now the Lord has given it to your son Absalom! At last you will taste some of your own medicine, you murderer!"

"Why should this dead dog curse my lord the king?"

Abishai demanded. "Let me go over and strike off his head!"

"No!" the king said. "If the Lord has told him to curse me, who am I to say no? My own son is trying to kill me, and this Benjaminite is merely cursing me. Let him alone, for no doubt the Lord has told him to do it. And perhaps the Lord will see that I am being wronged and will bless me because of these curses."

[Later:]

As the king was crossing [the Jordan River en route back to his throne], Shimei fell down before him, and pleaded, "My lord the king, please forgive me and forget the terrible thing I did when you left Jerusalem; for I know very well how much I sinned. That is why I have come here today, the very first person in all the tribe of Joseph to greet you."

Abishai asked, "Shall not Shimei die, for he cursed the Lord's chosen king!"

"Don't talk to me like that!" David exclaimed. "This is not a day for execution but for celebration! I am once more king of Israel!"

Then, turning to Shimei, he vowed, "Your life is spared." (2 Sam. 16:5-12; 19:18-23)

And now this word to all of you: You should be like one big happy family, full of sympathy toward each other, loving one another with tender hearts and humble minds. Don't repay evil for evil. Don't snap back at those who say unkind things about you. Instead, pray

for God's help for them, for we are to be kind to others,
and God will bless us for it. (1 Pet. 3:8-9)

I nsults thrive within the family better than anywhere else.
Why is that?

1. *People know each other well enough to know where to attack.*
After all, they live with each other. Day after day, week after
week, they see who's habitually messy or late or lazy. There
are plenty of targets for blasting.

2. *They know they can get away with it.* Unlike the workplace,
where a smart mouth can get you fired; or a social circle,
where friends can decide never to speak to you again, family
members *have* to keep living under one roof. "Ah, well, I was
just kidding," they rationalize. "She'll get over it."

3. *Television has raised the art of family sarcasm to a high level.*
It's the stock material of many a sitcom. The joy of zingers is
greatly relished in today's media.

The Bible's view, on the other hand, is to ignore insults.
That wouldn't make for very lively TV banter. But it would
make for healthier, safer homes.

King David was attacked at one of his weakest moments,
as he was being driven out of his capital by a rebellious son.
He was so stressed that he even wondered whether God was
behind Shimei's ranting (hardly!). But he still managed to
hold his tongue. He kept Abishai from retaliating.

And in time, his restraint was rewarded. Shimei apolo-
gized, and no blood was shed.

We will never prevent insults from flying, especially in
today's sharp-edged society. But we can stop the boomerang

effect, where one sarcastic crack evokes another, and another, and another. All we have to do is . . . say nothing.

Lord, this is hard for me—very hard. I confess that sometimes I even enjoy putting family members down. Forgive me for that, and change my heart to one of love and tenderness.

DOING THE WORD

In your mind, replay a typical put-down or wisecrack that has come your way recently—and practice saying nothing in return. Get the feel of halting the barrage by refusing to continue. Then do it in real life!

NOT ALWAYS FUN

Some Greeks who had come to Jerusalem to attend the Passover paid a visit to Philip, who was from Bethsaida, and said, "Sir, we want to meet Jesus." Philip told Andrew about it, and they went together to ask Jesus.

Jesus replied that the time had come for him to return to his glory in heaven, and that "I must fall and die like a kernel of wheat that falls into the furrows of the earth. Unless I die I will be alone—a single seed. But my death will produce many new wheat kernels—a plentiful harvest of new lives. If you love your life down here—you will lose it. If you despise your life down here—you will exchange it for eternal glory.

"If these Greeks want to be my disciples, tell them to come and follow me, for my servants must be where I am. And if they follow me, the Father will honor them." (John 12:20-26)

*S*acrifice—it's a noble-sounding word. Jesus knew that unless he submitted to personal sacrifice, he could not achieve his goal: "a plentiful harvest of new lives" (v. 24). The price, however, was excruciating.

In a much smaller way, we as parents face a call to sacrifice. There are times when the work of raising new, young lives is not fun. We spend money that we'd hoped to enjoy ourselves on necessities for the children. We give up sleep to be on duty during the night. We hold our temper when everything within us wants to explode. Parenting is at times an experience of dying—dying to selfish goals and personal desires.

In the rough and violent 1930s in Chicago, the Mafia's membership included a slick lawyer they called Artful Eddie because he was so good at keeping Al Capone out of jail. Time after time, he outwitted the authorities. But Eddie was also the father of a boy named Butch, and deep inside he knew his crime career would severely limit Butch's opportunities in the future. What else could the son do but follow in his father's footsteps?

Finally, the man made a fateful choice. He squealed on Capone. *Why?* the cops wanted to know. "I want to give my son a break," Eddie answered, and this time he wasn't being artful.

Not many weeks later, the mob silenced him forever with two shotgun blasts. Butch, however, went on to apply to Annapolis, and because his father had cleared the family name, he was accepted. In World War II he was the Navy's number-one ace, the first naval aviator ever to win the Congressional Medal of Honor. A few years later, they christened a new Chicago airport after him, and today nearly every traveler in North America knows his name: O'Hare. Instead of going down in history as despicable and vile, the family is remembered with pride.

What are you willing to sacrifice for your children?

Lord Jesus, I thank you that you died for me. I find it hard sometimes to give up my rights, my options, my assets for others. Help me to grasp what you meant when you said that loving my life is a good way to lose it, while despising my life will in fact result in future glory.

APPLYING THE WORD

Imagine a friend of yours is fed up with the limitations of marriage or parenting. "I'm missing all the fun, the travel, the freedom—this life is *so* confining!" the person wails. What would you say? How would you shed a new light on the situation?

BOUNDARIES ARE NOT BAD

God's laws are perfect. They protect us, make us wise, and give us joy and light. God's laws are pure, eternal, just. They are more desirable than gold. They are sweeter than honey dripping from a honeycomb. For they warn us away from harm and give success to those who obey them. (Ps. 19:7-11)

Oh, that you had listened to my laws! Then you would have had peace flowing like a gentle river, and great waves of righteousness. (Isa. 48:18)

Scolding and spanking a child helps him to learn. Left to himself, he brings shame to his mother. . . . Discipline your son and he will give you happiness and peace of mind. (Prov. 29:15, 17)

Wait a minute. Just *what* is it that offers us protection, makes us wise, gives us joy, success, happiness, peace of mind . . . is a better deal than gold, a more delicious taste than honey?

Rules! Boundaries! Limits!

Your child might hotly disagree, and at times you might, too. Rules, in our permissive era, stand for constraint, discomfort, no fun. Wouldn't it be great to have total *freedom!* says modern society.

Not really. Imagine standing on the observation deck of the World Trade Center in New York, 111 stories above the street, gazing out at the skyline. Now imagine standing there on a dark, inky night, a stiff wind blowing off the Atlantic into your face—*and no guardrails.* You have freedom to walk wherever you like.

In such a setting, one of two things will probably happen. You will either freeze in your tracks, afraid to move—or you will kill yourself.

Boundaries are not bad. Especially when they are God's boundaries, clearly but lovingly enforced by a mature adult.

Several years ago television newscaster Ted Koppel told a graduating class at Duke University,

> We have actually convinced ourselves that
> slogans will save us. Shoot up if you must, but use a
> clean needle. Enjoy sex whenever and with whomever
> you wish, but wear a condom. No! The answer is No!
> Not because it isn't cool or smart or because you might
> end up in jail or dying in an AIDS ward, but No because
> it's wrong, because we have spent five thousand years
> as a race of rational human beings . . . searching for truth
> and moral absolutes. In its purest form, truth is not a po-
> lite tap on the shoulder. It is a howling reproach. What

Moses brought down from Mount Sinai were not the Ten Suggestions.

Of course, it takes more than rules to make a family run smoothly. It also takes love, warmth, relationship. The following equations illustrate:

All rules, no relationship = a jail.

All relationship, no rules = a zoo.

Rules within relationship = a home.

Lord, thank you for loving me enough to draw
some boundaries for me, and then to enforce
them. Help me to do the same for my children.

DOING THE WORD

Put down on paper your own house rules, the patterns you require of those who live under your roof. You may be surprised at how *few* you can think of—probably less than two dozen. Post them on the refrigerator so you and your offspring both know what's expected. Then enforce them.

JUST DO IT

Listen to me, my son! I know what I am saying; *listen!* Watch yourself, lest you be indiscreet and betray some vital information. For the lips of [another man's wife (marginal reading)] are as sweet as honey, and smooth flattery is her stock in trade. But afterwards only a bitter conscience is left to you, sharp as a double-edged sword. She leads you down to death and hell. For she does not know the path to life. She staggers down a crooked trail and doesn't even realize where it leads.

Young men, listen to me, and never forget what I'm about to say: *Run from her! Don't go near her house,* lest you fall to her temptation and lose your honor, and give the remainder of your life to the cruel and merciless; lest strangers obtain your wealth, and you become a slave of foreigners. Lest afterwards you groan in anguish and in shame when syphilis consumes your body, and you say, "Oh, if only I had listened! If only I had not demanded my own way! Oh, why

50

wouldn't I take advice? Why was I so stupid? For now I must face public disgrace."

Drink from your own well, my son—be faithful and true to your wife. Why should you beget children with women of the street? Why share your children with those outside your home? Be happy, yes, rejoice in the wife of your youth. Let her breasts and tender embrace satisfy you. Let her love alone fill you with delight. (Prov. 5:1-19)

The popular culture says, "Adultery spices up your life." "A little walk on the wild side is exciting." "Why not?" The fantasies of our times are etched on a current sign in the gift shops—Wanted: Meaningful Overnight Relationship.

There's no such thing, claims the above Scripture passage, written by a king who knew plenty about sex. Adultery does not enliven; it *kills*. What does it kill? Trust. Whenever a husband and a wife can no longer count on each other, deadness has set in, along with suspicion, fear, and hostility.

Even physical death is possible in this age of the STD epidemic: the number of new sexually transmitted viruses and other dangers grows every year. The language of verses 11-13—"Lest afterwards you groan in anguish and in shame when syphilis consumes your body, and you say, 'Oh, if only I had listened! If only I had not demanded my own way! Oh, why wouldn't I take advice? Why was I so stupid? For now I must face public disgrace'"—is not so dramatic after all.

Of course, many of us read this text and shrug. *Nothing there for* me *to worry about*, we think. *I'd never do such a thing.*

But a wise speaker has said, "Marriage is like driving on a

mountain road. The ground beneath may be solid granite—but you're still only a few feet from the drop-off."

The final paragraph in verses 15-19 explains the antidote to temptation: Build an exciting and sensuous sex life *inside* of marriage. The Bible's words are almost embarrassing to our Western ears. After all, this is the one kind of sex we *don't* see on television and at the movies: passionate, happy, safe, *married* sex.

Maybe God's plan is the wild side after all. Maybe he knows more about long-term ecstasy than Hollywood does. After all, he thought up the idea of male and female in the first place, and we can best enjoy his invention by doing it his way.

Lord, I made you a promise the day of my wedding. I said I would keep myself wholly for my spouse, forsaking all others. I intend to keep that promise. And thanks for showing how to make the intimate life truly alive and fulfilling.

REINFORCING THE WORD

Get out your wedding script, or recording, or video . . . and review just what you pledged to your spouse that day. Read or listen to the words again. What did you say? Have you kept your word? Will you keep it from this point on?

NEVER TOO RUSHED

And now a man named Jairus, a leader of a Jewish synagogue, came and fell down at Jesus' feet and begged him to come home with him, for his only child was dying, a little girl twelve years old. Jesus went with him, pushing through the crowds.

As they went a woman who wanted to be healed came up behind and touched him, for she had been slowly bleeding for twelve years, and could find no cure (though she had spent everything she had on doctors). But the instant she touched the edge of his robe, the bleeding stopped.

"Who touched me?" Jesus asked.

Everyone denied it, and Peter said, "Master, so many are crowding against you. . . ."

But Jesus told him, "No, it was someone who deliberately touched me, for I felt healing power go out from me."

When the woman realized that Jesus knew, she began

to tremble and fell to her knees before him and told why she had touched him and that now she was well.

"Daughter," he said to her, "your faith has healed you. Go in peace."

While he was still speaking to her, a messenger arrived from Jairus' home with the news that the little girl was dead. "She's gone," he told her father; "there's no use troubling the Teacher now."

But when Jesus heard what had happened, he said to the father, "Don't be afraid! Just trust me, and she'll be all right."

When they arrived at the house, Jesus wouldn't let anyone into the room except Peter, James, John, and the little girl's father and mother. The home was filled with mourning people, but he said, "Stop the weeping! She isn't dead; she is only asleep!" This brought scoffing and laughter, for they all knew she was dead.

Then he took her by the hand and called, "Get up, little girl!" And at that moment her life returned and she jumped up! "Give her something to eat!" he said. Her parents were overcome with happiness. (Luke 8:41-56)

Notice how the needs of the junior-high-age girl have to compete with adult needs here. The girl is dying—but there's a grown-up who's pressing for assistance, too.

And notice which one prevails. After all, the woman has been hemorrhaging for as long as the girl has been *alive* (twelve years). So the grown-up manages to take precedence, while the crucial minutes tick away. . . .

Some things never change.

Young people today often come out on the short end of a priority list. Why? Because they're less articulate; they don't know how to present their needs with eloquence. They're just kids. They have no leverage, except to act in unacceptable ways that embarrass adults into noticing them.

The most important part of this story, however, is that while others may give up on the girl, Jesus does not. When everyone else is saying, "It's no use; it's too late," Jesus speaks words of confidence: "Don't be afraid! Just trust me, and she'll be all right" (v. 50). He presses on. Even a crowd of adults moaning and complaining cannot dissuade him from focusing on a young person in need. The result: a life reborn.

Back in verse 46, Jesus explained that "power" (Greek: *dunamis,* from which we get our English words *dynamite* and *dynamic*) "has gone out from me" toward the adult woman's body. She had been touched by the supernatural. The same *dunamis* was brought back for an encore in the girl's bedroom.

Young people, especially adolescents, need to encounter the power of God. They need a radicalizing experience that lets them know this Christian thing is more than just a head game. It's something real, dynamic, strong—in today's parlance, awesome.

No matter how busy, distracted, or disgruntled we adults become, our Lord is forever concerned about helping twelve-year-olds.

Lord, guide me in putting my kids as high on the agenda as you do. And show them what a strong God you truly are.

REFLECTING ON THE WORD

Imagine that Jesus Christ came to visit *your* child's bedroom! What would he say? Would he reprimand your son or daughter for clothes left lying on the floor, for an unmade bed? Or would he reach out his hand with a touch of new life? Next time you go to your child's bedroom, do something Jesus would have done.

GRIPE, GRIPE, GRIPE

The people were soon complaining about all
their misfortunes, and the Lord heard them. His anger
flared out against them because of their complaints, so
the fire of the Lord began destroying those at the far end
of the camp. They screamed to Moses for help, and
when he prayed for them the fire stopped. Ever after, the
area was known as "The Place of Burning," because the
fire from the Lord burned among them there.

Then the Egyptians who had come with them began to
long for the good things of Egypt. This added to the dis-
content of the people of Israel and they wept, "Oh, for a
few bites of meat! Oh, that we had some of the delicious
fish we enjoyed so much in Egypt, and the wonderful cu-
cumbers and melons, leeks, onions, and garlic! But now
our strength is gone, and day after day we have to face
this manna!"

Moses said to the Lord, "Why pick on me, to give me
the burden of a people like this? Are they *my* children?

Am I their father? Is that why you have given me the job of nursing them along like babies until we get to the land you promised their ancestors? Where am I supposed to get meat for all these people? For they weep to me saying,'Give us meat!' I can't carry this nation by myself! The load is far too heavy! If you are going to treat me like this, please kill me right now; it will be a kindness! Let me out of this impossible situation!"

The Lord sent a wind that brought quail from the sea and let them fall into the camp and all around it! As far as one could walk in a day in any direction, there were quail flying three or four feet above the ground.

But as everyone began eating the meat, the anger of the Lord rose against the people and he killed large numbers of them with a plague. So the name of that place was called, "The Place of the Graves Caused by Lust," because they buried the people there who had lusted for meat and for Egypt. (Num. 11:1-6, 11-15, 31, 33-34)

Don't grumble about each other, brothers. Are you yourselves above criticism? For see! The great Judge is coming. He is almost here. [Let him do whatever criticizing must be done.] (James 5:9)

I sn't it delicious to hear Moses, the saintly man of God, just *lose it* for once?! He may have been noted for his meekness (see Num. 12:3, KJV)—but on this particular day, he is *fried*, and he lets God know exactly how he feels. He wants out of his parenting role, thank you very much, over and done, "I *quit!*"

What precipitates such an eruption? Grumbling, griping, complaining. Every parent knows the feeling. You put up with about so much, and then you sense your control starting to slip away.

What kids and adults alike need to learn is that complaining is a *reaction* to events, and while many events cannot be controlled, *reactions can.* So many things in family life have no clear cause; they just *are.* Snowstorms, the flu, heavy traffic on the way to Grandma's, crowded bathrooms on Sunday morning. . . . Complaints won't change a thing. So why waste the energy?

A wise mother once raised her brood with the tart comment, "Some people would gripe if they were in heaven." Probably so. Here on earth grumbling is just as pointless, and as we learn to *cope with* adversity instead of complain about it, we do our families a great favor. (We also stay out of trouble with the Judge.)

Lord, I imagine at least one thing in my life is going to go wrong today. Help me to control my mouth when it happens and to react constructively instead.

REFLECTING ON THE WORD

Recall in your mind the last couple of complaints you voiced at your house. What triggered them? (In Moses' case, it was not having the right groceries on hand. What about you?) Did your complaints help the situation? Next time the same things happen (and they most assuredly will), how might you respond differently? What would do the *most good?*

NOT GOOD

And God said, "Let there be light," and there was light. *God saw that the light was good.*

God called the dry ground "land," and the gathered waters he called "seas." *And God saw that it was good.*

The land produced vegetation: plants bearing seed according to their kinds and trees bearing fruit with seed in it according to their kinds. *And God saw that it was good.*

God made two great lights . . . to govern the day and the night, and to separate light from darkness. *And God saw that it was good.*

God created the great creatures of the sea . . . and every winged bird according to its kind. *And God saw that it was good.*

God made the wild animals according to their kinds, the livestock according to their kinds, and all the creatures that move along the ground according to their kinds. *And God saw that it was good.*

God saw all that he had made, *and it was very good.*
The Lord God took the man and put him in the Garden of Eden to work it and take care of it. . . . The Lord God said, "It is *not* good for the man to be alone. I will make a helper suitable for him." . . . Then the Lord God made a woman. (Gen. 1:3-4, 10, 12, 16, 18, 21, 25, 31; 2:15, 18, 22, NIV, emphasis added)

Throughout the six days of creation, the Almighty is on a roll. Everything he touches turns out spectacular. Light and darkness, soil and water, plants and trees, fish and fowl, land animals great and small, then finally Adam himself . . . it's all "good"—"good"—"good"—"good"—"very good."

Then in chapter 2, something breaks the litany. God surveys his landscape and zeroes in on a problem. Despite the magnificent mountains, colorful peacocks, exquisite wildflowers, and rushing streams, a frown crosses his face as he says for the first time in human history, even before the Fall: "It is *not* good . . ." *What is it* that deserves such reproach? Disease? Violence? Blasphemy?

No, nothing that dramatic. Just *aloneness. Isolation.*

God immediately did something corrective. He created woman, thereby bringing about the option of marriage, companionship, togetherness.

We all need interaction. Our best ideas need feedback. Our deepest feelings need an outlet. Especially if we want marriage to be a partnership of souls, not just an economic or sexual alliance.

How tragic that a man as intelligent as Socrates once said,

62

"I can think of no person to whom one talks less than his wife." *Not good.*

But in our century we can hardly claim to have mastered the art of verbal intimacy. Says Dr. John Baucom: "With the appearance of the two-bathroom home, Americans forgot how to cooperate. With the appearance of the two-car family we forgot how to associate, and with the coming of the two-television home, we will forget how to communicate." *Not good.*

The din of children and media, the drain of hurried schedules, and the fear of conflict—they all take their toll, pushing us into more aloneness. Such isolation in a marriage does not trigger an instant crisis. It's not a bombshell like, say, adultery. It is rather like the slow, steady buildup of cholesterol in the arteries, choking the flow of nourishment to the limbs and organs and brain. But it can prove lethal.

Let every one of us who, like Adam, has been given "a suitable helper" cherish the companionship with loving words and deeds. Let us make time to share our lives, our dreams, our hopes, our fears. Let us bear each other's burdens and relieve each other's pain. That is, after all, God's original idea.

Lord, thank you for conceiving the
whole idea of marriage—a man and a woman
sharing life and love together, forever.
You could have arranged life on this planet
any number of other ways—but you didn't.

*Thank you for my spouse. May he or she never
feel alone because of my inattention.*

DOING THE WORD

Get out your calendar and plan a getaway with your spouse. It doesn't have to be expensive; you may be able to borrow lodging from a relative or friend; you might even trade houses with another couple to hold down costs. A full weekend would be nice, but just twenty-four hours can be effective. Give your attention solely to each other in fun, relaxation, romance, talking about topics you never seem to get around to in normal life, Scripture reading, and prayer.

BEYOND SCOLDING

> And now a word to you parents. Don't keep
> on scolding and nagging your children, making them
> angry and resentful. Rather, bring them up with the lov-
> ing discipline the Lord himself approves, with sugges-
> tions and godly advice. (Eph. 6:4)

> Fathers, don't scold your children so much
> that they become discouraged and quit trying. (Col. 3:21)

For the first year and a half of life, human babies enjoy a wonderful outpouring of praise. Mothers and fathers alike engage in smiling, cooing, tickling, playing, singing (even if they can't sing), and generally affirming the infant. Even messy diapers and projectile vomiting don't seem to cool the parental love fest. "That's all right, darling . . . you're still my sweetheart."

Then, just as the child gets to the point of understanding English and figuring out what all the soothing compliments *mean*—the level of happy talk plummets! His parents moan about the "terrible twos" and begin to fill his days with "No! Stop that! Don't touch the stereo! Oh, what in the world am I going to do with you, kid?"

Affirmation exits stage right. On comes nagging and scolding.

Children don't thrive very well under a constant barrage of correction. In that regard they are similar to adults. How many of us would keep working for a boss who criticized us 60 or 70 percent of the time?

The New International Version renders the above Scripture from Ephesians as follows: "Fathers, do not *exasperate* your children." (emphasis added). That is admittedly a hard rule to obey 365 days a year. But who of us would not agree that causing exasperation in a child is usually counterproductive? It seldom achieves the results we sought in the first place.

Instead, it leads to resentment, which if compounded can settle into bitterness. From there the trail is not far to depression. Yes, even the young can grow depressed.

And beyond that malady lies full-blown despair of ever pleasing Dad or doing anything right in life. For a few, there is one more step downward, and it is frightful: suicide.

Instead of nagging, the Bible advises loving discipline and godly suggestion. The apostle does not say to do *nothing* or become entirely permissive and laissez-faire. Replace the harangues, he says, with clear *positives*.

A seasoned principal whose elementary school was known for its order and achievement said, "With each incoming student, regardless of his or her past history, I start from the premise of 'You're a good kid, and I'm glad you're here in my school. We're going to have a good year together!' Now of course, some kids don't exactly merit that confidence, but I start out on the upbeat anyway. I can always deal with problems later. And it's amazing how many students match up to my initial expectations!"

How much more should a Christian parent, having been given a precious gift of life from the Father above, spend the majority of time affirming and encouraging.

Lord, I really need to be more positive
with my children. After all, I say I love them!
Help me to see them again with the wonder
and appreciation I felt when they were
first born. Help me to build up, not tear down,
just as you do for me.

DOING THE WORD

Go to a card shop, pick out something that says "I'm proud of you," and actually mail it to your child. Kids adore getting mail, and when they open the envelope to find an upbuilding message from Mom or Dad, they'll remember it a long time.

WHY THE GOOD TIMES ROLL

He who loves money shall never have enough. The foolishness of thinking that wealth brings happiness! The more you have, the more you spend, right up to the limits of your income. So what is the advantage of wealth—except perhaps to watch it as it runs through your fingers! The man who works hard sleeps well whether he eats little or much, but the rich must worry and suffer insomnia. (Eccles. 5:10-12)

Beware that in your plenty you don't forget the Lord your God and begin to disobey him. For when you have become full and prosperous and have built fine homes to live in, and when your flocks and herds have become very large, and your silver and gold have multiplied, that is the time to watch out that you don't become proud and forget the Lord your God who brought you out of your slavery in the land of Egypt. Beware that you don't forget the God who led you through the great and terrible wilderness with the dangerous snakes and scorpions, where it was so hot and dry. He gave you water from the rock! He fed you with manna in the wilderness (it was a kind of bread unknown before) so that you would become humble and so that your trust in him would grow, and he could do you good. He did it so that you would never feel that it was your own power and might that made you wealthy. Always remember that it is the Lord your God who gives you power to become rich, and he does it to fulfill his promise to your ancestors.

But if you forget about the Lord your God and worship other gods instead, and follow evil ways, you shall certainly perish, just as the Lord has caused other nations in the past to perish. That will be your fate, too, if you don't obey the Lord your God. (Deut. 8:11-20)

> But whatever is good and perfect comes to us from God, the Creator of all light, and he shines forever without change or shadow. (James 1:17)

B reathes there a husband or wife who doesn't think life would be *so much easier* with just a modest amount of extra money? They could get out of debt, trade cars, start orthodontia for the kids, plan a real vacation . . . if only their ship would come in. If only God would smile on them in a financial way.

The trouble is, most of us already have more than we had

five years ago. Certainly more than ten. And definitely more rooms in our house and gadgets in our kitchen than our parents or grandparents had at a comparable stage of marriage.

So, are we happier? More secure? More godly as a result?

Think back to your tougher days, your personal equivalent of "the great and terrible wilderness" of which God reminded the Israelites. Remember how he carried you along, how he provided food and protection?

Now read Deuteronomy 8:17-18 again: "He did it so that you would never feel that it was your own power and might that made you wealthy. Always remember that it is the Lord your God who gives you power to become rich, and he does it to fulfill his promise to your ancestors." These brilliant Scriptures teach us that bringing home a paycheck is *not* the result of our college degree, or good luck, or smart networking among our contacts, or even hard effort. All those things are but gifts from above, which come together to produce earnings. The Lord giveth, and the Lord can certainly take away; blessed be his name in either case.

Money is perhaps one of our greatest tests in life. It reveals our understanding of place: our place vis-à-vis God's place. So long as we grasp the truth that having money is a result of God's generosity toward us, he can keep the dollars coming. As soon as we start thinking we've pulled ourselves up by our bootstraps, he may remove his hand and let us thud back to the ground.

Lord, I thank you for blessing my
household with the ability to earn.

Let me never take it for granted.
Let me never forget the true
Source of my funds.

REFLECTING ON THE WORD

Dig out a financial reminder of how you made ends meet at least ten years ago, preferably more: a tax return, a household budget record, or even photos of those earlier days. (If you can't come up with any of these, ask your spouse to help you remember.) Look at how little your earnings were. How did you manage not to starve?! Then ask yourself: *Are we as contented now as we were then? Has the additional money helped us draw closer to God or not? Are there lessons to be learned by contrasting the two points of our lives?*

WHEN
SICKNESS STRIKES

Is anyone among you suffering? He should keep on praying about it. And those who have reason to be thankful should continually be singing praises to the Lord.

Is anyone sick? He should call for the elders of the church and they should pray over him and pour a little oil upon him, calling on the Lord to heal him. And their prayer, if offered in faith, will heal him, for the Lord will make him well; and if his sickness was caused by some sin, the Lord will forgive him.

Admit your faults to one another and pray for each other so that you may be healed. The earnest prayer of a righteous man has great power and wonderful results. (James 5:13-16)

Sickness just goes with the parenting territory. From infants' ear infections to kindergartners' chicken pox to teenagers' bronchitis . . . to far more serious maladies like broken bones, asthma, and juvenile diabetes . . . worried parents have ample reasons to seek out this passage of Scripture.

Despite the wonders of modern medicine, we find ourselves coping with pain and fever on a regular basis. When a child is sick, the whole rhythm of the household is upset. There's *more* work to be done, more need for empathy and compassion, more chance for misunderstanding. Other siblings don't want to stay as quiet as the sick person would prefer. The calendar has to be rearranged—appointments canceled, parties postponed. And while a mom or dad is concentrating on the one in bed, the other children seem to get away with murder as far as behavior goes.

The words of James, who had seen his half brother, Jesus, heal many a desperate person, can make a great difference in how we handle sickness in our homes. The apostle shows us four ways to be effective in praying for the sick:

1. *"Keep on praying" (v. 13).* Don't just pray once. Kneel beside the child's bed repeatedly . . . when he's awake, when he's asleep. Soak the situation in prayer. It's not an insult to God to ask him more than once.

2. *Take the initiative in asking church leaders to join you (v. 14-15).* Don't expect them to read your mind. Call and ask for help. Even if this isn't the tradition in your church, it is certainly biblical. Take James 5 at face value.

3. *Clean the relational slate between yourself and your spouse and children (v. 16).* Apologize for those half-hidden offenses that need to be talked about. God, apparently, is less interested in blessing people who don't get along with each other. Take the first step toward an open and contrite heart.

4. *Be "earnest" (v. 16) about your praying.* Don't just go through the motions. Don't dwell on your doubts about unanswered prayer. Truly *expect* God to act; after all, he is your loving Father. He doesn't enjoy sickness any more than you do. He hates all works of the enemy. Join him in a determined partnership to overcome this illness.

John Donne, the brilliant English poet best known for his "No man is an island" passage, spent the entire winter of 1623 in bed with a persistent illness. Yet during that ordeal he wrote a devotional book that included this: "Pray in thy bed at midnight, and God will not say, 'I will hear thee tomorrow upon thy knees at thy bedside'; pray upon thy knees there then, and God will not say, 'I will hear thee on Sunday at church.' God is no tardy God, no presumptuous God; prayer is never unseasonable; God is never asleep, nor absent."

Lord, I don't understand everything about divine healing. I am, frankly, perplexed at times when you seem not to answer. But I will not let my questions turn me into a cynic who says you probably won't heal so I shouldn't bother asking. You are a good God. And so, whenever sickness invades my house, you'll be hearing from me!

DOING THE WORD

Fold down the corner of this page or attach a yellow Post-It note so you can quickly find this reading the next time sickness strikes your home. Then follow what it says.

FAMILY SECRETS

Meanwhile the crowds grew until thousands upon thousands were milling about and crushing each other. He turned now to his disciples and warned them, "More than anything else, beware of these Pharisees and the way they pretend to be good when they aren't. But such hypocrisy cannot be hidden forever. It will become as evident as yeast in dough. Whatever they have said in the dark shall be heard in the light, and what you have whispered in the inner rooms shall be broadcast from the housetops for all to hear!" (Luke 12:1-3)

Now I am sending for many fishermen to fish you from the deeps where you are hiding from my wrath. I am sending for hunters to chase you down like deer in the forests or mountain goats on inaccessible crags. Wherever you run to escape my judgment, I will find you and punish you. For I am closely watching you, and I see every sin. You cannot hope to hide from me. (Jer. 16:16-17)

O God, you know so well how stupid I am, and you know all my sins. O Lord God of the armies of heaven, don't let me be a stumbling block to those who trust in you. O God of Israel, don't let me cause them to be confused. (Ps. 69:5-6)

"Τhis family is *so* hypocritical!" a teenager rages. "We all dress up and go to church looking so righteous, but if other people actually *lived* here, they'd find out otherwise."

A burst of adolescent steam? Or the truth? Parents should not be too quick to assume the first. Maybe the kid is putting his finger on something that needs attention.

In some dysfunctional homes, however, a child would not dare to be so blunt. The adult children of alcoholics often tell about the three unspoken rules of growing up: "Don't talk. Don't trust. Don't feel." In other words, keep a lid on it; maintain the image; pretend the shouting and insulting and hitting didn't happen; above all, don't let it get to your emotions.

Jesus told his disciples that hypocrisy and secrets won't stay buried forever. Things whispered have a way of getting "broadcast from the housetops for all to hear." Substance abuse comes out. So does adultery. So does homosexuality. So does battering. So does incest.

And so do a number of other sins we consider less serious but which are nonetheless damaging to family health. They won't stay behind the couch or in the attic. They have to be confessed, admitted, talked about, and turned from.

Phillips Brooks, eminent Episcopal bishop in the late 1800s

and author of the beloved Christmas carol "O Little Town of Bethlehem," wrote:

"Keep clear of concealment. Keep clear of the *need* of concealment. It is an awful hour when the first necessity of hiding anything comes. Where there are eyes to be avoided and subjects which must not be touched, then the whole bloom of life is gone."

When you and I get to the end of life, how will our spouses and children remember us? It really doesn't matter if they say we were wealthy or smart or even successful. But if they use words like *honest* and *believable* and *open*, we will have a legacy of which to be proud.

Lord, I confess I've been trying to ignore my problem with ＿＿＿＿＿＿＿＿＿＿＿. I now drop
(FILL IN THE BLANK)
my guard and ask your forgiveness. My family needs me to talk about this too. That scares me—but I will try to come clean with them as well. Give me courage, I pray.

DOING THE WORD

If the above prayer applies to you, resolve now to speak with the appropriate family members *by the end of this week.*

THE FINE ART OF PEACEMAKING

When others are happy, be happy with them. If they are sad, share their sorrow. Work happily together. Don't try to act big. Don't try to get into the good graces of important people, but enjoy the company of ordinary folks. And don't think you know it all!

Never pay back evil for evil. Do things in such a way that everyone can see you are honest clear through. Don't quarrel with anyone. Be at peace with everyone, just as much as possible.

Dear friends, never avenge yourselves. Leave that to God, for he has said that he will repay those who deserve it. [Don't take the law into your own hands.] Instead, feed your enemy if he is hungry. If he is thirsty give him something to drink and you will be "heaping coals of fire on his head." In other words, he will feel ashamed of himself for what he has done to you. Don't let evil get the upper hand, but conquer evil by doing good. (Rom. 12:15-21)

Try to stay out of all quarrels, and seek to

live a clean and holy life, for one who is not holy will not see the Lord. (Heb. 12:14)

[Christ] never answered back when insulted; when he suffered he did not threaten to get even; he left his case in the hands of God who always judges fairly. (1 Pet. 2:23)

D iplomacy, they say, is the art of letting the other person have it your way. It is an art sorely needed not only in the United Nations and the halls of Congress, but also at our kitchen tables and in the halls of our homes.

A step beyond diplomacy (negotiation, compromise) lies true peacemaking. What household couldn't use more of that?

The above passages give us some keys to developing this priceless skill:

1. *Empathize with family members (Rom. 12:15).* Feel what they're feeling; see the situation from behind their eyes for a change. Think of more than just your own agenda.

2. *Come down off your adult pedestal—"enjoy the company of ordinary folks" (Rom. 12:16).* Could that possibly include six-year-olds? Ten-year-olds? Thirteen-year-olds?

3. *Stop keeping score, remembering who did what to whom, carrying grudges.* Jesus didn't. He got the rawest deal of all, and yet his attitude was basically, "Let it go; let the Father take care of my persecutors, whenever he gets around to it. It's not my job." It takes two to argue. A one-sided quarrel doesn't work. So let the barbs and insults pass. Many, many irritations in life simply need to be *ignored.*

4. *The final key is in Romans 12:20—surprise your antagonist*

with a gift! The metaphor of "heaping coals of fire on his head" makes no sense to us today, but in ancient Palestine it was vivid and powerful. Most homes used wood or charcoal for heating and cooking. If your fire went out overnight or by neglect, there were no handy matches or lighter fluid to bail you out. You had to get live coals from somebody else. And how would you carry them? In a bucket on your head, of course, like you carried everything else!

What this Scripture says is that if your enemy comes sheepishly looking for warm coals because his cooking fire has died out, don't slam the door in his face and yell, "Tough luck, buddy!" Be generous with him; heap the glowing coals into his bucket and send him on his way with kindness. He will be astounded at the turn of events.

And you will have established a new reputation for peacemaking.

The standard atmosphere in our homes does *not* have to be contentious and argumentative. We *can* let the peace of God prevail. It starts in our own hearts.

Lord, too often the harsh words fly and the tempers rise at my house. Teach me to be a peacemaker. Help me be part of the solution instead of part of the aggravation.

DOING THE WORD

What tense situation or relationship in your life needs a surprise, a coals-of-fire gesture? Make a plan, and then follow through.

LET'S MOVE
(LET'S NOT)

How dare you tell me, "Flee to the mountains for safety," when I am trusting in the Lord?

For the wicked have strung their bows, drawn their arrows tight against the bowstrings, and aimed from ambush at the people of God. "Law and order have collapsed," we are told. "What can the righteous do but flee?"

But the Lord is still in his holy temple; he still rules from heaven. He closely watches everything that happens here on earth. He puts the righteous and the wicked to the test; he hates those loving violence. He will rain down fire and brimstone on the wicked and scorch them with his burning wind.

For God is good, and he loves goodness; the godly shall see his face. (Ps. 11)

Have you ever gotten fed up with your family's circumstances and wanted to just rent a truck, pack up overnight, and head for Wyoming (or Delaware, or Alaska)?

"Any neighborhood would be better than this one!" you tell yourself. "I can't stand *[pick one or more]* the noise, the heat, the traffic, the kind of friends my kids are choosing, the school system, the taxes, the crime—*let's move."*

Especially as the nation becomes more and more urban, greater numbers of us long for country living, a simpler, less hurried lifestyle . . . open space for our children to run and play . . . quieter days and fewer temptations (we assume). With less and less respect in America for common decency, let alone Christian values, some people even think about emigrating. But where would be better?

Fleeing, says David, is not the answer. The answer is to remind ourselves of the one who "still rules from heaven" (v. 4). He hasn't moved half an inch, nor has he fallen asleep. He's watching every traffic jam, every schoolyard fight, every violent mugging, every permissive vote in every legislature. He has promised to put *everyone* to an ultimate test, both "the righteous and the wicked" (v. 5). Will you and I qualify to "see his face"?

When we North American Christians get upset with our lot, we need to remember our brothers and sisters in places like the Ukraine. For seventy years Ukrainian believers raised godly offspring in a hostile setting. How did they manage? Every morning they got their children ready for school and said, "Now today you'll be told there is no God, that prayer is a joke, that church is a foolish exercise, that our pastor is a social parasite—but you know better. Hold on to the truth. Greater is he that is in you than he that is in the Soviet system."

The cure for our frustration is not out there somewhere. It

is in the character of God, who loves us and instills within us the fortitude to stand when life appears to be collapsing.

---

*Lord, you are pure goodness in the
midst of a wretched society.
Strengthen our family on the
inside to stand for you.*

DOING THE WORD

Pick out *one arena* in which you could make a difference where you live. It may be the neighborhood school, the community association, or an outreach to troubled teens. Make some phone calls, and come up with a way to show the love of Christ in that context.

PEACE OR PANIC?

"So my counsel is: Don't worry about *things*—food, drink, and clothes. For you already have life and a body—and they are far more important than what to eat and wear. Look at the birds! They don't worry about what to eat—they don't need to sow or reap or store up food—for your heavenly Father feeds them. And you are far more valuable to him than they are. Will all your worries add a single moment to your life?

"And why worry about your clothes? Look at the field lilies! They don't worry about theirs. Yet King Solomon in all his glory was not clothed as beautifully as they. And if God cares so wonderfully for flowers that are here today and gone tomorrow, won't he more surely care for you, O men of little faith?

"So don't worry at all about having enough food and clothing. Why be like the heathen? For they take pride in all these things and are deeply concerned about them.

But your heavenly Father already knows perfectly well
that you need them, and he will give them to you if you
give him first place in your life and live as he wants you to.

"So don't be anxious about tomorrow. God will take
care of your tomorrow too. Live one day at a time."
(Matt. 6:25-34)

Isn't it part of a mother's official job description to *worry?*
Can you be a diligent parent *without* spending part of each
day (or night) brooding over the hazards? Like . . .

What if your child's cough turns into something serious?

How will you ever pay for college?

Is the teacher putting anti-Christian ideas into your child's
head?

Why are the mealtime arguments getting more common—
or are they?

Will this sibling rivalry never stop? They sound like they
want to *kill* each other!

What if your source of income dries up?

Is your son doing drugs behind your back?

What does your daughter's boyfriend *really* want?

This Scripture says that such stewing is essentially heathen
in nature (v. 31). What an odd rebuke! How so?

Heathens are people who don't recognize the presence of
a loving God. They assume they are alone in the world. No
one is looking out for them but *them.* Hence, they worry
about food, clothing, and a thousand other things.

Those who know a good and kind heavenly *Father* (notice
the parent term in verses 26 and 32) and in fact "give him
first place" in their lives (v. 33) have a tremendous ally in the

parenting task. They look at parents in the animal kingdom (v. 26) and see that things do have a way of working out, don't they? Generation follows generation, as it has from the days of Eden. God is intensely interested in the succession of the human race and more than willing to take care of its problems when invited to do so.

Worried parents are tense parents. They keep themselves and everyone around them on edge. As a result, their households don't laugh very much. They don't relax. They fall short of God's abundant, joyous life.

This is not to say that we can doze off and stop paying attention to our job. There *are* dangers in the world, both for us and for our children. But there is a greater God. What he asked us to start, he will help us complete—with a sense of peace, not panic.

---

*Lord, when I grow afraid, when I wake up
consumed with apprehension, when I let the
circumstances of family life upset me . . .
remind me of the birds and the field lilies.
Assure me that you still love my children.
You won't let us fall. Help me transfer what I
know in my head to my emotional core.
Let me live just this one day
in your warm embrace.*

DOING THE WORD

Over the next week, start keeping a list of all the worries that cross your mind. As you write them down, some of them will reveal their inherent foolishness. So be it! Each day, pray through the accumulating list, handing the items over to God one by one. Let him relieve your load of anxiety, and rest in his goodness.

Do As I Do

"The Lord your God told me to give you all these commandments which you are to obey in the land you will soon be entering, where you will live. The purpose of these laws is to cause you, your sons, and your grandsons to reverence the Lord your God by obeying all of his instructions as long as you live; if you do, you will have long, prosperous years ahead of you. Therefore, O Israel, listen closely to each command and be careful to obey it, so that all will go well with you, and so that you will have many children. If you obey these commands, you will become a great nation in a glorious land 'flowing with milk and honey,' even as the God of your fathers promised you.

"O Israel, listen: Jehovah is our God, Jehovah alone. You must love him with *all* your heart, soul, and might. And you must think constantly about these commandments I am giving you today. You must teach them to your children and talk about them when you are at

home or out for a walk; at bedtime and the first thing in
the morning. Tie them on your finger, wear them on
your forehead, and write them on the doorposts of your
house!" (Deut. 6:1-9)

If you were Jewish, this second paragraph would be your
John 3:16—the core statement of your faith. Called the
Shema in Hebrew, it declares who God is, how to respond to
him, and how to raise children who will do the same. No
wonder pious Jews recite it twice a day.

What is further remarkable is the *sequence* of Moses' instructions:

Directive A: Love God intensely and think about his commandments constantly.

Directive B: Teach your kids, in a variety of ways, to do the
same.

It does little good to jump into B if you're not doing A. You
can't impress on your offspring what you yourself don't
possess. If the adult spiritual life is not growing and thriving,
there's not much use trying to make little boys and girls
more godly.

Many classes and sermons for parents seem to start with
verse 7: "You must teach them to your children." The message is "Come on, you moms and dads—get busy teaching
your children about God. . . . The Christian home is of ut-
most importance. . . . Build the 'family altar' with your children. . . ." Such exhortings should include a preface based on
verses 5-6.

As young people see that God is truly *real* to their parents,
that the Bible is worth reading on ordinary Tuesdays, that

prayer is as natural as breathing, that God's rules are taken seriously and followed consistently, they will believe the declarations that come from parental lips. They will do as they have seen done.

Susanna Wesley, it is said, had a curious way of praying amid her duties of raising and home-schooling eleven children. She would sit on a kitchen chair and pull her long apron up over her face and head—thus letting her brood know that she was not to be bothered while she spoke with God! She didn't wait till they were asleep or out of the house. She let her devotion to God take center stage.

No wonder she produced two sons—John and Charles—who shook the British and American world of the 1700s with a mighty revival called Methodism. The children embraced what their parents demonstrated.

O God, make me more than just a
noisy gong and clanging cymbal to my kids.
Let them sense reality in what I say
about you because of the way I live.

DOING THE WORD

Review your own devotional discipline. Is it consistent? How would your children describe your personal walk with God? How would you *like* them to describe it? Make plans accordingly.

TAKING CHARGE

Take a lesson from the ants, you lazy fellow. Learn from their ways and be wise! For though they have no king to make them work, yet they labor hard all summer, gathering food for the winter. But you—all you do is sleep. When will you wake up? "Let me sleep a little longer!" Sure, just a little more! And as you sleep, poverty creeps upon you like a robber and destroys you; want attacks you in full armor. (Prov. 6:6-11)

You know your children are making headway when they start taking *independent responsibility* for time and resources. When the bed gets made without a reminder from you, when the homework is tackled ahead of the deadline, when the allowance is *not* all spent in the first twenty-four hours . . . you can rejoice that your offspring are indeed growing up!

The values of planning, rolling out of bed on time, and tackling unexciting duties may be slow in coming. Kids may also relapse from time to time; the diligent fourth-grader turns into a slouch in junior high. But after all, even we adults are inconsistent sometimes, needing to return for a lesson from the industrious, self-motivated ant.

For both young and old, the poverty and want that trail the lazy person are no fun. How important it is to learn early in life the importance of following through, doing a thorough job, and making oneself useful. Kids who learn these lessons will, in fact, grow up to be terrific parents!

Lord, help me to be a good "ant" today,
so my kids can get the picture of Proverbs 6.

DOING THE WORD

Write a list of five things you ought to accomplish this week. Show the list to your child (thus creating some pressure on yourself). Then cross the items off as you complete them— and let your child see your progress.

ONE SMALL COMPLIMENT FOR ANANIAS AND SAPPHIRA

But there was a man named Ananias (with his wife Sapphira) who sold some property and brought only part of the money, claiming it was the full price. (His wife had agreed to this deception.)

But Peter said, "Ananias, Satan has filled your heart. When you claimed this was the full price, you were lying to the Holy Spirit. The property was yours to sell or not, as you wished. And after selling it, it was yours to decide how much to give. How could you do a thing like this? You weren't lying to us, but to God."

As soon as Ananias heard these words, he fell to the floor, dead! Everyone was terrified, and the younger men covered him with a sheet and took him out and buried him.

About three hours later his wife came in, not knowing what had happened. Peter asked her, "Did you people sell your land for such and such a price?"

"Yes," she replied, "we did."

And Peter said, "How could you and your husband even think of doing a thing like this—conspiring together to test the Spirit of God's ability to know what is going on? Just outside that door are the young men who buried your husband, and they will carry you out too."

Instantly she fell to the floor, dead, and the young men came in and, seeing that she was dead, carried her out and buried her beside her husband. Terror gripped the entire church and all others who heard what had happened. (Acts 5:1-11)

Wretched, despicable Ananias and Sapphira—con artists who got royally caught, scum of the New Testament. They couldn't resist the thrill of pats on the back for donating *all* their equity in a liquidated piece of real estate, when in fact it was only part. . . .

But—we might give them credit for one small virtue. At least they were unified, as a married couple, on a financial decision. They had talked it over and come to a joint conclusion on how to handle their money.

That's more than can be said for many of us. The vast majority of modern husbands and wives hate to talk about finances. They say it just ends up in an argument; the other party is *so dense* about these things; why can't he or she understand that money doesn't grow on trees; we can't afford everything we'd like; blah, blah, blah. So one spouse ends up making unilaterial decisions while the other sulks.

One of the keys to marital harmony is accepting the concept of *OUR money*. Not *my* money (because I happened to earn it) or *your* money, but *ours*. We manage to say "our kids," "our refrigerator," "our TV." Why not "our money"?

The dollars are all a gift from above, anyway. And (to get to the main point of this Scripture) the God who gave us the ability to acquire money in the first place does not like people trying to hoodwink him. It's not smart to "conspir[e] together to test the Spirit of God's ability to know what is going on" (v. 9).

That's about as clever as trying to fool a bank's ATM with a piece of cardboard. Or trying to stump a NASA scientist on algebra. It doesn't work.

Neither does giving money at church to impress others. Or rationalizing various and sundry expenses under the category of tithe—things that mainly benefit us while bearing some slight connection to the Lord's work, if you think real creatively about it.

The couple who fudges together falls together. The couple who plans together and gives with an open and honest spirit receives God's smile.

Lord, the only reason I have any financial assets
at all is because you've enabled me. I really want
to give as freely and joyfully as you do.

DOING THE WORD

In a time of prayer with your spouse, open your checkbook ledger before the Lord and ask him, "What do you think?" Examine together, in light of God's perspective, how you've been spending money.

INNOCENT VICTIM

Time went by and the child grew and was weaned; and Abraham gave a party to celebrate the happy occasion. But when Sarah noticed Ishmael—the son of Abraham and the Egyptian girl Hagar—teasing Isaac, she turned upon Abraham and demanded, "Get rid of that slave girl and her son. He is not going to share your property with my son. I won't have it."

This upset Abraham very much, for after all, Ishmael too was his son.

But God told Abraham, "Don't be upset over the boy or your slave-girl wife; do as Sarah says, for Isaac is the son through whom my promise will be fulfilled. And I will make a nation of the descendants of the slave-girl's son, too, because he also is yours."

So Abraham got up early the next morning, prepared food for the journey, and strapped a canteen of water to Hagar's shoulders and sent her away with their son. She walked out into the wilderness of Beersheba, wandering aimlessly.

When the water was gone she left the youth in the
shade of a bush and went off and sat down a hundred
yards or so away. "I don't want to watch him die," she
said, and burst into tears, sobbing wildly.

Then God heard the boy crying, and the Angel of God
called to Hagar from the sky, "Hagar, what's wrong?
Don't be afraid! For God has heard the lad's cries as he is
lying there. Go and get him and comfort him, for I will
make a great nation from his descendants."

Then God opened her eyes and she saw a well; so she
refilled the canteen and gave the lad a drink. And God
blessed the boy and he grew up in the wilderness of
Paran, and became an expert archer. And his mother
arranged a marriage for him with a girl from Egypt.
(Gen. 21:8-21)

An old African proverb says, "When the elephants fight,
the grass gets trampled." Nowhere is that more true
than in an exploding marriage with children present. The big
people fight, argue, threaten, scream, and sue, while the little
people wince in silence, absorbing the bulk of the pain.

Ishmael did nothing to deserve this trauma, other than to act
like any normal sixteen-year-old boy with a squalling half
brother in the house. Suddenly the party came to a crashing
halt, Sarah was yelling at his father, who got equally upset . . .
and by the next morning, Ishmael and his mother were told to
pack up and get out. Abraham, a wealthy man with abundant
resources, provided them with nothing more than a sack
lunch and a canteen as he ushered them out of his life!

Millions of boys and girls today know exactly how Ishmael

felt. *It's not fair*, they whimper as they cry themselves to sleep in a dingy apartment, if not a welfare hotel or even an aging car. Grown-ups whom they have always trusted have suddenly turned and disappeared, all their *I-love-you*s vanishing into thin air. The reasons make no sense at all. And in a very short matter of time, like Hagar and Ishmael in the desert, they are reduced to desperation.

It is reassuring to know that the angel of the Lord sees every young victim of divorce, every panicky single mom. When sinful people destroy the family, God hears and makes a way. He is indeed "a father to the fatherless" (Ps. 68:5), "a tested help in times of trouble" (Ps. 46:1). He not only salvages the present but even plans for the future.

"I don't want to watch him die," Hagar wailed. Neither did God. He loved Ishmael and wanted him to grow up, marry, have children, and become a success. Toward that end, God met his immediate need for water and started the stabilizing process. He is still today in the business of rescuing children in distress.

Lord, help me to love children the way you do (even someone else's). Show me any children in my circle of influence to whom you want me to reach out. And thank you for being the kind of God who always keeps caring.

REFLECTING ON THE WORD

Ask yourself, *Am I doing* anything—*even something small—that's having a harmful effect on my children?*

"You Make Me So Mad!"

A wise man controls his temper. He knows that anger causes mistakes. (Prov. 14:29)

A rebel shouts in anger; a wise man holds his temper in and cools it. (Prov. 29:11)

Finishing is better than starting! Patience is better than pride! Don't be quick-tempered—that is being a fool. (Eccles. 7:8-9)

If you are angry, don't sin by nursing your grudge. Don't let the sun go down with you still angry—get over it quickly; for when you are angry, you give a mighty foothold to the devil. (Eph. 4:26-27)

My dear brothers, take note of this: Everyone should be quick to listen, slow to speak and slow to become angry, for man's anger does not bring about the righteous life that God desires. (James 1:19-20, NIV)

Return to the Lord your God, for he is gracious and merciful. He is not easily angered; he is full of kindness and anxious not to punish you. (Joel 2:13)

By now you should be thoroughly guilt-ridden about the scores of times your family members have made you furious!

It is a small comfort, however, to notice that the Bible doesn't declare anger totally out of bounds. Paul says in Ephesians that if you get steamed, try to get over it quickly. James advises being *"slow* to become angry." Even God himself, according to the prophet Joel, "is not *easily* angered."

That means he does get ticked off sometimes. More than a few times, in fact, according to the Old Testament and even the New. His children did something outrageous or defiant, and God's temperature rose.

So does ours when kids break heirloom china, sass us back, lose house keys, or ditch their coats in frigid weather. "What is the matter with you!" we start to shriek. "If you had half a brain . . ." Soon our temples are pounding, the child is crying (or glowering), and everybody wants to change his last name.

At such a moment, it helps to remember the very pragmatic words of Scripture, which teach that *responding in anger usually doesn't achieve what we want.* It's counterproductive. It only aggravates an already tense situation. It "causes mistakes," says Proverbs 14:29. Every sports coach knows that: the angry player can't think straight and ends up committing fouls or errors. So do angry parents.

While our forebears sometimes stifled anger to the point of extremity, our modern generation has swung to the opposite side, popping off about every little thing in the name of being honest about our feelings. Scripture doesn't seem to be terribly worried that we'll harm our health by stuffing our fury. It leans in the direction of self-control, of letting offenses pass without rebuttal, of leaving vengeance to God.

And here's the most sobering thought of all: Our kids will learn to vent their anger as little or as much as they see us do it! That is all the more reason to model "the righteous life that God desires."

Lord, my kids can really get under my skin
sometimes. Grant me your inner peace,
so that I won't do foolish things. Help me to be
less concerned about my rights than about
staying in control and being an effective
manager of the situation.

REFLECTING ON THE WORD

Think back to the last time you lost your temper over a family situation. What did your outburst achieve? Were you satisfied with the result? How might you have reacted differently and achieved more? Finally, what will you do the next time this circumstance comes up?

The Soft Side of Fathering

[God] is like a father to us, tender and sympathetic to those who reverence him. For he knows we are but dust and that our days are few and brief, like grass, like flowers, blown by the wind and gone forever. (Ps. 103:13-14)

"See, I will send you another prophet like Elijah before the coming of the great and dreadful judgment day of God. His preaching will bring fathers and children together again, to be of one mind and heart." (Mal. 4:5-6)

But you know that Timothy has proved himself, because as a son with his father he has served with me in the work of the gospel. (Phil. 2:22, NIV)

We talked to you as a father to his own children—don't you remember?—pleading with you, encouraging you and even demanding that your daily lives should not embarrass God but bring joy to him

who invited you into his Kingdom to share his glory.
(1 Thess. 2:11-12)

What's a dad like? Tradition says he's tough, reserved, unemotional, aloof, someone to be respected, feared—and left alone.

These passages say something quite different.

None of the four speak about fathering directly; they all *use* fathering to comment on something else.

In the first passage, God is compared to a dad who knows full well that his kids are far from perfect—and doesn't seem too upset about it. He freely cuts them some slack.

In the second, the gap between dads and kids is shown to be crossable; they can be reunited by strong preaching that calls them to softness, unity, and even repentance.

The third shows that a dad and his son can have as much respect and admiration for each other as did Paul and Timothy.

The fourth illustrates a dad *getting involved* with his children, talking to them, caring about their spiritual lives, even getting emotional at times about how they're doing. He doesn't dismiss this as women's work.

North American Christians have a tradition of the praying mother who faithfully brings her brood before the Lord no matter how far they stray. Southern gospel music even has tunes with titles such as "Mother's Prayers Have Followed Me."

Why don't we ever hear about the praying father? Why is there no corresponding image of *Dad* on his knees, calling out to God for his sons and daughters? Of Dad making warm and gentle contact (even a hug?) with his children? Of Dad choking up with pride—or, conversely, with concern—over events in his kids' lives?

If we are looking for the full range of what fathering is all about, the Scriptures hold the best clues.

O Perfect Father in heaven, help me (or my husband) in learning to be more like you. Free us all from cultural stereotypes in order to do what our kids need most.

DOING THE WORD

If you're a father, spend ten minutes on your knees discussing each of your children *by name* with the Lord. Ask what this particular child needs most from you, and listen to the divine suggestions. Then follow through.

THE SCANDAL

Noah became a farmer and planted a vineyard, and he made wine. One day as he was drunk and lay naked in his tent, Ham, the father of Canaan, saw his father's nakedness and went outside and told his two brothers. Then Shem and Japheth took a robe and held it over their shoulders and, walking backwards into the tent, let it fall across their father to cover his nakedness as they looked the other way. When Noah awoke from his drunken stupor, and learned what had happened and what Ham, his younger son, had done, he cursed Ham's descendants. (Gen. 9:20-25)

Whose heart is filled with anguish and sorrow? Who is always fighting and quarreling? Who is the man with bloodshot eyes and many wounds? It is the one who spends long hours in the taverns, trying out new mixtures. Don't let the sparkle and the smooth taste of strong wine deceive you. For in the end it bites like a poisonous serpent; it stings like an adder. You will see hallucinations and have delirium tremens, and you will say foolish, silly things that would embarrass you no end when sober. You will stagger like a sailor tossed at sea, clinging to a swaying mast. And afterwards you will say, "I didn't even know it when they beat me up. . . . Let's go and have another drink!" (Prov. 23:29-35)

If ever a man had earned the right to a pedestal, it was Noah. The early accolades in Genesis 6 are downright effusive: He "was a pleasure to the Lord . . . the only true righteous man living on the earth at that time. He tried always to conduct his affairs according to God's will" (vv. 8-10).

His sons respected him enough to follow him into the ark. The townspeople could scoff if they wanted; their father held more credibility. Once the rain began to fall and the big barge began to float, their amazement could no doubt be seen on their faces. *Dad's right! God IS judging the world, and we're going to be spared.*

Then, when the Flood was all over, when Noah's renown could not be higher, the last scene of his biography finds him humiliating himself with drunkenness. Like a baseball pitcher who carries a no-hitter into the eighth inning and then suddenly erupts into an argument over balls and strikes, until the umpire has to evict him from the field . . . like a war hero bedecked with medals who returns to hometown parades and a million-dollar book contract, only to get caught molesting little boys . . . this ancient hero of the faith lurches into a pit of embarrassment and shame. His own sons have to figure out how to save Dad's dignity.

The Bible does not hide this ugly event from us. (For an

even more sordid family mess involving alcohol, see Genesis 19:30-38, the story of Lot and his two daughters.) The warning from Proverbs 23 is equally vivid. The biggest problem with drinking is not that it's expensive or that it makes you gain weight. The scary part is that it too often leads to *a loss of control*—which is something no parent can afford. Young eyes are watching, and when they see Dad or Mom out of control, their entire world shudders.

It is true that the Bible does not totally condemn the use of alcoholic beverages. It is also clear, however, that drunkenness is wrong—not funny, not an excusable lapse, not an unfortunate happenstance—but morally wrong.

There's something else that's clear in our day, and that is that our culture has a *major* problem with alcohol abuse. Every weekend, drinking is destroying families; drinking is breaking trust (not to mention occasional limbs, jaws, and skulls). As in the case of Noah's family, it doesn't have to be. This kind of human tragedy can be avoided by clearheaded parents who will say no and choose to keep their reputation intact.

Lord, I've worked too hard at earning the respect of my children to blow it with any kind of substance abuse. Help me show them the clear advantages of staying in control at all times.

REINFORCING THE WORD

Give your family a verbal explanation of your personal convictions about alcohol. (If, as you're thinking of what to say, you find that your position isn't supportable, then revise it!)

REPUTATION CHECK

The character of even a child can be known by the way he acts—whether what he does is pure and right.

If you must choose, take a good name rather than great riches; for to be held in loving esteem is better than silver and gold. (Prov. 20:11; 22:1)

Don't let anyone think little of you because you are young. Be their ideal; let them follow the way you teach and live; be a pattern for them in your love, your faith, and your clean thoughts. (1 Tim. 4:12)

Credit bureaus may not start tracking youngsters until they reach age eighteen, but others certainly do. Neighbors, relatives, teachers, and college admissions officers pay attention to how "even a child" performs. So do their peers—and parents.

In other words, it's never too soon for a child to be

thinking about *reputation*. The adult who makes excuses for childish selfishness or irresponsibility, who says, "Boys will be boys," does no favor. It is entirely proper for children to be made to care about the impression they make on others.

In the wake of misconduct, a quiet parental word of "I'm disappointed in your behavior" or "I'm surprised at you" can often be more effective than a full-blown harangue. Raising children to be conscious of their image—especially in the sight of God—is entirely biblical.

Of course, what's good for kids is good for adults, too. That is why integrity is so important for parents. When children know that we do the right thing whether we are being watched or not, they tend to do likewise. If they see us cut corners, fudge the truth, or take financial advantage of others, they are not likely to seek a higher road.

So we are all in this reputation challenge together. Young and older, our goal should be the words of Colossians 1:10—"that the way you live will always please the Lord and honor him, so that you will always be doing good, kind things for others, while all the time you are learning to know God better and better."

------

*Lord, I truly want you to be proud of me. Keep
me today from embarrassing you in any way.
Help me teach my children to care about what
you think as well. If we please you, our human
reputation will certainly take care of itself. May
we bring honor to your name in the world.*

DOING THE WORD

While driving in the car with your child, ask him or her these questions:

- "What would you say about the reputation of *[name a best friend]*? Do kids and teachers generally think well of him or her, or not?"
- "If this person wanted a better reputation, what should he or she do?"
- "What do you think about *my* reputation? Go ahead—be honest!"
- "How do you think people feel about your reputation?"
- "What would really make the Lord proud of you and me?"

GET ALL YOU CAN,
CAN ALL YOU GET?

Then someone called from the crowd, "Sir, please tell my brother to divide my father's estate with me."

But Jesus replied, "Man, who made me a judge over you to decide such things as that? Beware! Don't always be wishing for what you don't have. For real life and real living are not related to how rich we are."

Then he gave an illustration: "A rich man had a fertile farm that produced fine crops. In fact, his barns were full to overflowing—he couldn't get everything in. He thought about his problem, and finally exclaimed, 'I know—I'll tear down my barns and build bigger ones! Then I'll have room enough. And I'll sit back and say to myself, "Friend, you have enough stored away for years to come. Now take it easy! Wine, women, and song for you!"'

"But God said to him, 'Fool! Tonight you die. Then who will get it all?'

"Yes, every man is a fool who gets rich on earth but not in heaven."

Then turning to his disciples he said, "Don't worry about whether you have enough food to eat or clothes to wear. For life consists of far more than food and clothes." (Luke 12:13-23)

A re rich families happier? Not necessarily, as this passage shows. Family assets have a way of causing family headaches.

The man's request in verse 13 seems fair enough; his father has died, and his sibling is now refusing to share (shades of boyhood days gone by?). What they need is a probate judge.

"Not I," says Jesus. "That's not my specialty. What *I* concentrate on is real living, not capital gains."

The story he goes on to tell about the rich farmer portrays, again, a man doing what seems prudent and wise. His business is booming, and so he'll launch an expansion program. Keep the ball rolling. Maximize the cash flow. Leverage the opportunities.

Yet God calls him a very strong epithet: "Fool!" We may naturally ask why. What was so bad about this man?

His focus was on getting rather than giving, on storing rather than sowing. Accumulation had become his sole goal. A better life for him was Priority Number One.

In God's eyes, that was a dead-end street, and he elected to make the point immediately. Death put a quick end to the man's building project. There would be no more harvests. Instead, the estate would be splintered.

Ephesians 4:28 reveals one of the strangest reasons in the

world for a person to work hard, to succeed on the job, to amass wealth: "that he may have something to share with those in need" (NIV). *Accumulate something—to share.* That's certainly not the curriculum at Harvard Business School. Neither is it the way most of us think. But it's God's plan.

Would you rather your children knew you as wealthy or generous? Both would be nice, of course—but if you had to choose one, which would it be? Whatever you select will most likely determine the one *they* select when they grow up. And once you're gone, how will they handle the dividing of *your* estate? The pattern for generations to come is yours to mold.

Lord, I'm more concerned what you think
of my life's ledger than what my banker thinks,
or my father-in-law, or anyone else.
Yet I should be honest enough to admit
I have a stingy, hoarding streak, too.
Help me to open my hand to those in need,
knowing that you smile every time I do.

DOING THE WORD

With your children, plan to surprise someone with a totally unexpected act of generosity. Give some money, food, or clothing anonymously, not because you were asked or because the calendar requires it (birthday, Christmas, etc.). Do something together that's entirely "hilarious" (2 Cor. 9:7).

DAY WITH A DIFFERENCE

"Remember to observe the Sabbath as a holy day. Six days a week are for your daily duties and your regular work, but the seventh day is a day of Sabbath rest before the Lord your God. On that day you are to do no work of any kind, nor shall your son, daughter, or slaves—whether men or women—or your cattle or your house guests. For in six days the Lord made the heaven, earth, and sea, and everything in them, and rested the seventh day; so he blessed the Sabbath day and set it aside for rest." (Exod. 20:8-11)

When he came to the village of Nazareth, his boyhood home, he went as usual to the synagogue on Saturday, and stood up to read the Scriptures. (Luke 4:16)

On every Lord's Day each of you should put aside something from what you have earned during the week, and use it for this offering. The amount depends on how much the Lord has helped you earn. (1 Cor. 16:2)

I f George Gallup took a poll on people's support for the Ten Commandments, most of the tenets would win handily. Modern adults would still endorse the ideas of honoring one's parents, no murder, no lying, no idols, no adultery (well, in theory anyway).

The biggest exception would be this thing about the Sabbath. Very outdated, people would say. A special holy day? Come on. Didn't that lead to all kinds of legalism, till it got so bad Jesus had to come along and knock out the commandment for good by doing all kinds of "forbidden" things on the Sabbath?

Well, not entirely. He did poke holes in the embellishments added to the rule books over the centuries. He criticized those who refused to help a needy person because it was the Sabbath. But in his own personal life, the day still meant something. Luke 4:16 tells us that going to worship was part of his weekly rhythm, "his custom" (KJV). He didn't stop to debate each weekend, *Shall I, or shall I not? I suppose I should go. On the other hand, the scheduled rabbi this week is rather boring. I've had a hard week; maybe some extra sleep would be just as beneficial. . . .*

He had set his pattern, and he stuck to it.

The apostle Paul similarly called for *giving* to be a regular, weekly occurrence. Not once in a while, when I'm feeling generous, when a financial windfall has happened to come along. Every payday, in proportion to what God has supplied, it is time to give.

If George Gallup were to come to your home and ask your children, "What's unique about Sunday at your house? Any traditions? Anything you *always* do? What's the atmosphere? How hectic or restful is it?" what answers would he hear? What patterns will your children use in building the next generation of families?

No one wants a return to the Sabbath legalism of years gone by. But the alternative should not be complete disregard of this special day. What conscious definition of the Lord's Day do you want to pass along to your children?

Lord, I truly do enjoy worshiping you, giving to you, serving, and resting. Now help me set a rhythm for my household.

DOING THE WORD

Write down three things you could do to make the Lord's Day smoother and more meaningful in your home.

PAY ATTENTION—
TO WHAT?

Only fools refuse to be taught. Listen to your father and mother. What you learn from them will stand you in good stead; it will gain you many honors.

Every young man who listens to me and obeys my instructions will be given wisdom and good sense. Yes, if you want better insight and discernment, and are searching for them as you would for lost money or hidden treasure, then wisdom will be given you and knowledge of God himself; you will soon learn the importance of reverence for the Lord and of trusting him.

My son, never forget the things I've taught you. If you want a long and satisfying life, closely follow my instructions. Never tire of loyalty and kindness. Hold these virtues tightly. Write them deep within your heart.

Young men, listen to me as you would to your father. Listen, and grow wise, for I speak the truth—don't turn away. For I, too, was once a son, tenderly loved by my mother as an only child, and the companion of my father. He told me never to forget his words. "If you follow them," he said, "you will have a long and happy life. *Learn to be wise,*" he said, "*and develop good judgment and common sense! I cannot overemphasize this point.*" Cling to wisdom—she will protect you. Love her—she will guard you. (Prov. 1:7-9; 2:1-5; 3:1-3; 4:1-6)

These kinds of Scriptures always evoke a hearty *Amen!* from parents. We *love* having the Bible back us up. If only our seemingly deaf kids would read these passages once a week and take them to heart. . . .

However, there is a message here for us too. Solomon *assumed* that fathers and mothers were, in fact, giving their offspring instructions and teaching to follow. He started from the premise that parents were actively inputting wisdom and guidance. (Not nagging. Not criticism. Not complaining about irresponsibility or stubbornness. Instead, positive direction . . . ways to succeed . . . ways to honor the Lord.)

The question is: *Are we?* Are our children getting this kind of benefit from us? If they felt inclined to actually obey Proverbs 1 and 2 and 3 and 4, to listen and learn the secrets of life from their parents—would there be anything to listen to?

Do you ever actually *say* things that resemble the lines of Proverbs? Or would you feel awkward doing so? If so, why? Do you think such talk is better left to ministers and Sunday school teachers?

Solomon didn't think so. Many of our grandparents didn't think so. They spoke unashamedly about the godly life, about what God expects of us, and how he will bless those who walk in his wisdom.

How are kids today supposed to figure all that out? Somebody has to articulate it. Public schoolteachers aren't allowed to do it. Television certainly won't. Our kids' peers aren't old enough to have learned it. The job is ours.

Lord, with all my heart I want my children to absorb insight and wisdom. Guide me in choosing the best words to use. Help me in giving them a clear path to follow.

DOING THE WORD

Stop to assess your various ways of instructing your children—both the formal, scheduled ways (family devotions, Scripture memory) and the informal, serendipitous ways (talks while riding in the car, talks at bedtime, etc.). How much is getting across? Do you need to step up the pace? If so, make definite plans to do so.

BACK TO SCHOOL

Work hard and cheerfully at all you do, just as though you were working for the Lord and not merely for your masters, remembering that it is the Lord Christ who is going to pay you, giving you your full portion of all he owns. He is the one you are really working for. And if you don't do your best for him, he will pay you in a way that you won't like—for he has no special favorites who can get away with shirking. (Col. 3:23-25)

This should be your ambition: to live a quiet life, minding your own business and doing your own work, just as we told you before. As a result, people who are not Christians will trust and respect you, and you will not need to depend on others for enough money to pay your bills. (1 Thess. 4:11-12)

Notebooks and pencils and gym socks—that's the least of it. The late-August scurry often includes new sneakers, registration fees, band instrument rentals, and maybe even a doctor's exam, until a mother's checkbook is empty and so is her gas tank.

But getting kids ready for another year of school entails even more than the physical. We also need to prepare their spirit, their attitude.

If school is in fact a young person's main occupation for now, then how should a Christian student work? The above Scriptures sound the important themes: Study both *hard* and *cheerfully* (do those two go together?!), as if the teacher were not Ms. Kowalski or Mr. Peterson, but the Great Teacher from Nazareth. Do your best . . . mind your own business . . . earn the respect of others . . . don't depend on others to carry you along. These themes—valid for both students and adults—show us how to live a life of excellence.

Christians, young and older, are people who give their best, *whether it's fun or not.* European history can be dull; so can balancing a household budget. But we press on, because we serve the Lord of both history and money.

Christians give their best *whether it's easy or not.* Mastering the parts of speech, multiplying fractions, sticking to a fitness program; every day has its challenges.

Christians give their best *whether it's expected or not.* A few schools and teachers, sad to say, have lost sight of excellence and now settle for mediocrity. The same is true of some bosses. But not the Lord Christ.

Christians give their best *whether it's popular or not.* Classmates may mock the A student. Coworkers may laugh at the employee who gives the extra effort a supervisor won't even notice. But sliding toward average is not worthy of Jesus.

A nineteenth-century British poet named John Oxenham wrote:

> To every man there openeth a way, and ways, and a Way:
>   And the high soul takes the high road
> And the low soul gropes the low.
>   And in between, on the misty flats,
> The rest drift, to and fro.
>   But, to every man there openeth a high way and a low;
> And every man decideth the way his soul shall go.

The point of both the poem and the words from Colossians and 1 Thessalonians is: Go for the high road. Aim for the top. You may not hit it, but whatever you do, don't waste your life on the misty flats.

That's solid advice for schoolchildren—and their parents.

Lord, I admit I go through a lot of days and
weeks assuming I work just for a human boss.
Thank you for reminding me that in the
ultimate sense, I serve you—and help me instill
that viewpoint in my children as well.

DOING THE WORD

Read these Scriptures and the Oxenham poem with your children. Talk about how school is going and what it means to be a *Christian* student. You might even memorize one of the verses—or the poem—together as a family.

ARE THE LIGHTS ON?

Follow God's example in everything you do just as a much loved child imitates his father. Be full of love for others, following the example of Christ who loved you and gave himself to God as a sacrifice to take away your sins. And God was pleased, for Christ's love for you was like sweet perfume to him.

Let there be no sex sin, impurity or greed among you. Let no one be able to accuse you of any such things. Dirty stories, foul talk, and coarse jokes—these are not for you. Instead, remind each other of God's goodness, and be thankful.

You can be sure of this: The Kingdom of Christ and of God will never belong to anyone who is impure or greedy, for a greedy person is really an idol worshiper—he loves and worships the good things of this life more than God. Don't be fooled by those who try to excuse these sins, for the terrible wrath of God is upon all those who do them. Don't even associate with such people.

For though once your heart was full of darkness, now it is full of light from the Lord, and your behavior should show it! Because of this light within you, you should do only what is good and right and true.

Learn as you go along what pleases the Lord. Take no part in the worthless pleasures of evil and darkness, but instead, rebuke and expose them. It would be shameful even to mention here those pleasures of darkness that the ungodly do. But when you expose them, the light shines in upon their sin and shows it up, and when they see how wrong they really are, some of them may even become children of light! That is why God says in the Scriptures, "Awake, O sleeper, and rise up from the dead; and Christ shall give you light."

So be careful how you act; these are difficult days. Don't be fools; be wise: make the most of every opportunity you have for doing good. Don't act thoughtlessly, but try to find out and do whatever the Lord wants you to. Don't drink too much wine, for many evils lie along that path; be filled instead with the Holy Spirit and controlled by him. (Eph. 5:1-18)

Of all the metaphors to describe the Christian essence, this is perhaps the best: *Light.* Jesus came as the Light of the World, and he calls us to be people of the Light. Our homes are ordained as beacons in a dark society that's fumbling and stumbling for direction.

Light doesn't shout and scream for attention. It doesn't pick fights. It just silently, steadily shines, and suddenly everybody knows what's real and what's not.

This passage lists the aspects of a well-lighted home: full of love (v. 2), doing "only what is good and right and true" (v. 9), learning what pleases the Lord (v. 10), exposing sin (vv. 11, 13), doing good at every opportunity (v. 16), being controlled by the Holy Spirit (v. 18).

It also outlines what darkness means: sex sin, impurity, greed (vv. 3, 5), dirty stories, foul talk, coarse jokes (v. 4), foolishness and thoughtlessness (vv. 16-17), abuse of alcohol (v. 18). Many a family has gotten hurt bumping into one or more of these in the dark.

We all work and shop and travel alongside people every day who are the epitome of darkness. Our kids go to school with classmates in real danger. Some of their teachers may be no better. But which is stronger—darkness or light? In a contest, which one wins? The light. The words of 1 John 4:4 ring out, "Greater is he that is in you, than he that is in the world" (KJV).

Let us not be afraid to be different from other houses on the block. Let us not fear to show the light. It surely beats the alternative.

---

*O Lord, my prayer is the song
by Graham Kendrick:*

*"Shine, Jesus, shine!
Fill this [home] with the Father's glory;
Blaze, Spirit, blaze!
Set our hearts on fire.
Flow, river, flow—
Flood the nations with grace and mercy;*

*Send forth your Word,
Lord, and let there be light."*

DOING THE WORD

On a piece of paper, measure the candlepower of your home according to this passage. Write down the aspects of a well-lighted home listed at the top of the previous page, and give each one an honest rating, from 150 watts (maximum) down to 100 . . . 75 . . . 60 . . . 40 . . . or even a tiny 15-watt refrigerator bulb! Ask the Lord how you might brighten up the rooms.

TIME TO BLOW THE WHISTLE

And have you quite forgotten the encouraging words God spoke to you, his child? He said, "My son, don't be angry when the Lord punishes you. Don't be discouraged when he has to show you where you are wrong. For when he punishes you, it proves that he loves you. When he whips you, it proves you are really his child."

Let God train you, for he is doing what any loving father does for his children. Whoever heard of a son who was never corrected? If God doesn't punish you when you need it, as other fathers punish their sons, then it means that you aren't really God's son at all—that you don't really belong in his family. Since we respect our fathers here on earth, though they punish us, should we not all the more cheerfully submit to God's training so that we can begin really to live?

Our earthly fathers trained us for a few brief years, doing the best for us that they knew how, but God's correction is always right and for our best good, that we may share his holiness. Being punished isn't enjoyable while it is happening—it hurts! But afterwards we can see the result, a quiet growth in grace and character. (Heb. 12:5-11)

Your child has messed up. In the face of clear instructions, your child has disobeyed. Your guidelines have been fractured. Now what will you do about it?

There are at least half a dozen good-sounding excuses to dodge the issue: (1) Discipline will just cause a family uproar. (2) My child will cry. (3) I'm quite busy just now. (4) Other parents let their kids do this all the time. (5) My child might hate me afterward. (6) There must have been extenuating circumstances. (7) My spouse could handle this better than I could. (8) I remember doing the same stunt when I was a kid. . . .

Hear the words of Scripture: "Any loving father does [this] for his children. Whoever heard of a son who was never corrected?" (v. 7). The example of our heavenly Father calls us to be firm. He knows there are times that demand a clear response: "You stepped across a line, and I cannot let that pass. The consequence for what you *chose* to do is _____."

Actually, the sooner the better. And the less emotional the better. Did you ever see a basketball referee moan and wring his hands as he called a pushing foul or a three-second violation? Not at all. He blows his whistle, states the facts, announces the penalty—and lets the *players* go hysterical! But they respect him (see v. 9), because deep down they know he's right.

We parents are in the business of building "grace and character" (v. 11). Through loving discipline, we chip away that which is ungraceful and devious. Following our tough-minded Father in heaven, we take action when it's needed, knowing full well there may be a noisy outcry. Our goal is not peace and quiet; it is growth and maturity.

Lord, when I feel like turning my head
and ignoring my child's behavior, remind me
to be like you. Give me courage to act.

DOING THE WORD

Think back to a recent episode when you did *not* provide character-building discipline. What should you have done? How could you have demonstrated loving correction? Keep your plan in mind, because you will no doubt need it before long!

Up from Zero

Jabez was more distinguished than any of his brothers. His mother named him Jabez because she had such a hard time at his birth (Jabez means "Distress").

He was the one who prayed to the God of Israel, "Oh, that you would wonderfully bless me and help me in my work; please be with me in all that I do, and keep me from all evil and disaster!" And God granted him his request. (1 Chron. 4:9-10)

What an awful name for the new baby! His mother is so exhausted after a long labor and delivery that she retaliates in anger: "Call him Distress! He's been nothing but a pain so far."

And how doubly terrible in the Israelite culture, where names and their meaning were far from casual. Your name cast the die for your entire life: remember Jacob ("the Trickster")? One commentator says Hebrew names were "regarded as possessing almost magic power."

Many people today also suffer from early hurts—if not from their name, then from parental rejection, from fetal alcohol syndrome, from bad nutrition, from any number of stresses. Some are indeed marked for life.

Not Jabez. He wasn't like the boy named Sue that Johnny Cash sang about, who "grew up quick and grew up mean . . . my fists got hard and my wits got keen, and I roamed from town to town to hide my shame . . . I vowed to kill that man who gave me that awful name." Deep within Jabez's soul, he yearned for God to help him overcome his rough start. He pled with the Lord to turn the tide, to help him overcome his name and all that it signified, to make him a success. He refused to be limited by his background, his stereotype. He would be *different* from his image. He would surprise people. He would seek God's blessing to break free from his past.

Such optimism God could not ignore. He fulfilled Jabez's fondest dreams.

Here in the midst of Scripture's dullest section (1 Chron. 1–9 reads like a telephone book!) pops up this inspiring vignette of one man, mentioned nowhere else in the Bible. He would not accede to disadvantage. His mother's word would not be the last. His God would push away the distress of his beginning and let him soar with eagles.

Thank you, Lord, that you can make
us into overcomers. Keep me from selling
myself short, because only you can decide
how far I will really go.

SHARING THE WORD

Do you know someone who got off to a rough start in life? Find an opportunity to share the story of Jabez with him or her.

ONE KEY FOR YOU, AND ONE FOR ME

Honor Christ by submitting to each other.
You wives must submit to your husbands' leadership in
the same way you submit to the Lord. For a husband is
in charge of his wife in the same way Christ is in charge
of his body the Church. (He gave his very life to take
care of it and be its Savior!) So you wives must willingly
obey your husbands in everything, just as the Church
obeys Christ.

And you husbands, show the same kind of love to
your wives as Christ showed to the Church when he
died for her, to make her holy and clean, washed by bap-
tism and God's Word; so that he could give her to himself as a glorious Church without a single spot or
wrinkle or any other blemish, being holy and without a
single fault. That is how husbands should treat their
wives, loving them as parts of themselves. For since a
man and his wife are now one, a man is really doing himself a favor and loving himself when he loves his wife!

No one hates his own body but lovingly cares for it, just as Christ cares for his body the Church, of which we are parts.

(That the husband and wife are one body is proved by the Scripture, which says, "A man must leave his father and mother when he marries so that he can be perfectly joined to his wife, and the two shall be one.") I know this is hard to understand, but it is an illustration of the way we are parts of the body of Christ.

So again I say, a man must love his wife as a part of himself; and the wife must see to it that she deeply respects her husband—obeying, praising, and honoring him. (Eph. 5:21-33)

Here is the Bible's most famous—and infamous—teaching on marriage. Christians for centuries have loved what it says to the opposite sex, while frowning at what it says to their own gender! Husbands wish their wives would read it more often. Wives wish their husbands would memorize it and take heed.

Maybe we all ought to stop pitching the text across the breakfast table or the car seat to each other and hear what it says to *us*.

The passage, in fact, is amazing for what it leaves out. It says nothing, for example, about communication in marriage. It makes only one oblique reference to sex. Nothing about money, or in-laws, or career building. Nothing about shared housework, weekend getaways, or decision making.

How could the apostle Paul omit such crucial instructions? Perhaps he has wisely cut to the heart of the matter for each gender—the toughest part, but also the single make-or-break issue—knowing that if a spouse will do *this one thing*, the rest will take care of itself.

For husbands, it is to *love*—to get emotionally involved with their wives, to care, to cherish. Most men find this a lot harder to do than the more outward things: paying the bills, fixing the leaky roof, keeping the car running properly. To love is to open up, to become vulnerable, to become wife-centered instead of self-centered. It is to embrace the emotional side of living, not just the pragmatic. It is to make a woman feel special. If you keep loving this woman, says Paul, you will reach the pinnacle of relationship, something comparable to the way Christ feels about his church.

The challenge for wives, of all the aspects Paul could have spotlighted, is to *submit*. Not to cook, to clean, to stay attractive, to converse intelligently, to provide thrills in bed, to succeed in business or volunteer efforts, to bear children or raise them with diligence. Most of these are likely to come naturally. The one call in Ephesians 5 is for wives to recognize that a home—like any human organization (school, corporation, city, state, nation)—must have leadership. It cannot run smoothly without guidance, with which the rest of the members must cooperate.

Yes, verse 21 says there are times for both parties to yield: "Honor Christ by submitting to each other." But this verse must not be so inflated as to block out the clear import of the dozen verses that follow. This passage says something very specific to married men and something else to married women. For all of us, our task is to concentrate on reading our own mail, not the other person's, and doing what it says.

----

*Lord, I recognize that you designed marriage
a certain way, and I will be happiest if I stick
to your plan. When I don't exactly feel like
doing what this passage says, soften my heart
and help me honor you by obeying your Word.
Let my spouse enjoy the benefits of living
with a godly, obedient partner.*

DOING THE WORD

Find the right quiet moment to ask your spouse the following risky question:

Husbands: "How am I doing at truly loving you? What could I do to make you feel more loved?"

Wives: "Are there ways I'm resisting you or making it difficult for you to lead our home?"

Then be still and listen to the answer.

Mother-in-Law's Secret

And Elimelech Naomi's husband died; and she was left, and her two sons.

And they took them wives of the women of Moab; the name of the one was Orpah, and the name of the other Ruth: and they dwelled there about ten years.

And Mahlon and Chilion died also both of them; and the woman was left of her two sons and her husband.

Then she arose with her daughters-in-law, that she might return from the country of Moab: for she had heard in the country of Moab how that the Lord had visited his people in giving them bread.

Wherefore she went forth out of the place where she was, and her two daughters-in-law with her; and they went on the way to return unto the land of Judah.

And Naomi said unto her two daughters-in-law, Go, return each to her mother's house: the Lord deal kindly with you, as ye have dealt with the dead, and with me.

The Lord grant that ye may find rest, each of you in

the house of her husband. Then she kissed them; and they lifted up their voice, and wept.

And Ruth said, Entreat me not to leave thee, or to return from following after thee: for whither thou goest, I will go; and where thou lodgest, I will lodge: thy people shall be my people, and thy God my God:

Where thou diest, will I die, and there will I be buried: the Lord do so to me, and more so, if aught but death part thee and me.

When she saw that she was stedfastly minded to go with her, then she left speaking unto her. (Ruth 1:3-9, 16-18, KJV)

Then Naomi her mother-in-law said unto her, My daughter, shall I not seek rest for thee, that it may be well with thee? (Ruth 3:1, KJV)

And the work of righteousness shall be peace; and the effect of righteousness, quietness and assurance for ever.

And my people shall dwell in a peaceable habitation, and in sure dwellings, and in quiet resting places. (Isa. 32:17-18, KJV)

The flowing poetry of verse 16—"Whither thou goest, I will go; and where thou lodgest, I will lodge"—makes most people think of wedding ceremonies: a dreamy bride promising to blend her future with that of her handsome Prince Charming.

In fact, the original setting for these words was quite different. They were spoken by a recently widowed daughter-in-law to her mother-in-law, also a widow.

Think about it a minute: Would you voluntarily follow your mother-in-law *anywhere?* Let alone to a foreign nation where you knew not a soul, there to share an apartment with her?

If today's humor and sarcasm are any indication, many young women wouldn't even follow their mother-in-law to a good sale at Tiffany's. The tensions and disagreements of in-law relationships are often handled by keeping a sizable distance from one another.

Ruth didn't *have* to do what she did. No law or custom required her to go with Naomi. Her sister-in-law, Orpah, didn't. Apparently Ruth wanted to. Why?

A possible answer emerges as we carefully note Naomi's language about home life. "The Lord grant you that ye may find *rest,* each of you in the house of her husband" (1:9, emphasis added). Later on, after they'd lived in Bethlehem for a while, she proposed to play matchmaker by quaintly saying, "My daughter, shall I not seek *rest* for thee, that it may be well with thee?" (3:1, emphasis added).

The words in Hebrew are *menuchah* and *manoach*—"place of rest." To Naomi, that's what made a home worth having. She wasn't concerned about how many rooms it had or whether the furniture was luxurious. Servants, children, entertainment—all the things we covet—were beside the point. A home was, at its core, a safe haven, a shelter from the storm, a place of love and rest.

Ruth had no doubt sensed this about Naomi's home before she ever married into the family. Here was a woman who knew how to set a climate of peace. Even after the jolt of her husband's death, and then both her sons', she maintained a home atmosphere that drew Ruth like a magnet. This place of rest was more attractive to Ruth than staying with her own relatives, hometown, and traditions.

In a stormy, argumentative world, we can give our families few gifts worth more than a home with a loving, restful atmosphere, a place where calm is the rule rather than the exception, a place characterized by God's peace. That will be more attractive to daughters-in-law, and everyone else, than the fanciest dinners or the most expensive gifts.

Lord, let your rest first of all prevail in
my heart and spread from there to my home.
I want people to sense the calm of Christ when
they step across my threshold. Point out to me
the things that needlessly churn me up.
Make me, as St. Francis prayed,
"an instrument of thy peace."

DOING THE WORD

On a piece of paper, write five practical changes you could make to increase the peacefulness of your home. Less television? Planning your schedules the night before? Getting out of bed on time? Playing quiet music during mealtimes? What else?

A FATHER'S INFAMY

Jeroboam's son Abijah now became very
sick. Jeroboam told his wife, "Disguise yourself so that
no one will recognize you as the queen, and go to Ahijah
the prophet at Shiloh—the man who told me that I
would become king. Take him a gift of ten loaves of
bread, some fig bars, and a jar of honey, and ask him
whether the boy will recover."

So his wife went to Ahijah's home at Shiloh. He was
an old man now and could no longer see. But the Lord
told him that the queen, pretending to be someone else,
would come to ask about her son, for he was very sick.
And the Lord told him what to tell her.

So when Ahijah heard her at the door, he called out,
"Come in, wife of Jeroboam! Why are you pretending to
be someone else?" Then he told her, "I have sad news for
you. Give your husband this message from the Lord
God of Israel: 'I promoted you from the ranks of the common people and made you king of Israel. I ripped the

kingdom away from the family of David and gave it to you, but you have not obeyed my commandments as my servant David did. His heart's desire was always to obey me and to do whatever I wanted him to. But you have done more evil than all the other kings before you; you have made other gods and have made me furious with your gold calves. And since you have refused to acknowledge me, I will bring disaster upon your home and will destroy all of your sons—this boy who is sick and all those who are well. I will sweep away your family as a stable hand shovels out manure. I vow that those of your family who die in the city shall be eaten by dogs, and those who die in the field shall be eaten by birds.'"

Then Ahijah said to Jeroboam's wife, "Go on home, and when you step into the city, the child will die. All of Israel will mourn for him and bury him, but he is the only member of your family who will come to a quiet end. For this child is the only good thing that the Lord God of Israel sees in the entire family of Jeroboam. And the Lord will raise up a king over Israel who will destroy the family of Jeroboam. Then the Lord will shake Israel like a reed whipped about in a stream; he will uproot the people of Israel from this good land of their fathers and scatter them beyond the Euphrates River, for they have angered the Lord by worshiping idol-gods. He will abandon Israel because Jeroboam sinned and made all of Israel sin along with him."

So Jeroboam's wife returned to Tirzah; and the child died just as she walked through the door of her home. And there was mourning for him throughout the land,

just as the Lord had predicted through Ahijah. (1 Kings
14:1-18)

I f you've ever puzzled over the second commandment—
that awesome threat from Mount Sinai about the sin of the
fathers being visited upon the children—here is a graphic
illustration. The jealous Lord God had made himself abundantly clear on the matter of idol worship, but King Jeroboam had sculpted his golden calves anyway. Now little
Abijah would pay the price.

Why?! we scream. *It's not fair! Let the headstrong father take
the heat for his own rebellion.*

No doubt when we get to heaven, we will probe this
question further with God around the great throne. For the
time being, however, the story stands as a stern warning not
to place our kids at risk by our own foolishness. When
parents incur the hot anger of a jealous Lord, children sometimes get scorched.

On more than one occasion, God has used the sickness or
death of a child as a megaphone through which to shout to a
spiritually deaf parent. Oblivious to every plea from spouse,
friend, and clergy, the wayward dad has finally sobered up
and heard God's call while staring into a tiny coffin. Jeroboam, however, was too tough to feel even this jolt; he
continued his reckless disobedience as long as he lived.

Meanwhile, what torment must have gone through his
wife's mind as she left Ahijah's house, the prophet's words
ringing in her ears: "When you step into the city, the child
will die." Did that mean she could prolong her son's life by
wandering in the countryside? Should she *never* go home

again? But then who would care for her son? Did she dare leave him to Jeroboam's mercies? What a catch-22!

In the end, by whatever tortured logic, she returned to Tirzah—and the prophecy proved deadly accurate.

We who bring children into the world are the guardians of their fate in more ways than we know. They are helpless, vulnerable, unaware. How crucial that we give them every chance not only to live but also to know what God requires and what he forbids. They will learn it best by watching our reverent submission to the Almighty.

---

*Lord, if you ever need to rap my knuckles about
something I'm doing wrong, deal with me
directly; please don't let my children suffer for
it. I'll listen, because I sincerely, deeply care
what you think about my lifestyle.*

REINFORCING THE WORD

Read the actual text of the Ten Commandments from Exodus 20:1-17. Is there anything in your life that could legitimately be called an idol—something you serve and love to the point that you wouldn't give it up?

UP CLOSE AND PERSONAL

About that time King Herod moved against some of the believers and killed the apostle James (John's brother). When Herod saw how much this pleased the Jewish leaders, he arrested Peter during the Passover celebration and imprisoned him, placing him under the guard of sixteen soldiers. Herod's intention was to deliver Peter to the Jews for execution after the Passover. But earnest prayer was going up to God from the church for his safety all the time he was in prison.

The night before he was to be executed, he was asleep, double-chained between two soldiers with others standing guard before the prison gate, when suddenly there was a light in the cell and an angel of the Lord stood beside Peter! The angel slapped him on the side to awaken him and said, "Quick! Get up!" And the chains fell off his wrists! Then the angel told him, "Get dressed and put on your shoes." And he did. "Now put on your coat and follow me!" the angel ordered.

So Peter left the cell, following the angel. But all the time he thought it was a dream or vision and didn't believe it was really happening.

After a little thought he went to the home of Mary, mother of John Mark, where many were gathered for a prayer meeting.

He knocked at the door in the gate, and a girl named Rhoda came to open it. When she recognized Peter's voice, she was so overjoyed that she ran back inside to tell everyone that Peter was standing outside in the street. They didn't believe her. "You're out of your mind," they said. When she insisted they decided, "It must be his angel. [They must have killed him.]"

Meanwhile Peter continued knocking. When they finally went out and opened the door, their surprise knew no bounds. He motioned for them to quiet down and told them what had happened and how the Lord had brought him out of jail. "Tell James and the others what happened," he said—and left for safer quarters. (Acts 12:1-9, 12-17)

You can bet that Rhoda, John Mark, and any number of other young people remembered *this* home prayer meeting for the rest of their lives!

The fledgling church was in a crisis. One apostle had already been brutally murdered. Now Peter was on death row. The only thing holding up his execution was that it happened to be Passover week, when normal Jerusalem life and activity shut down. Government offices were closed; heavy restrictions applied. But as soon as the sun went down

Saturday evening, the execution squad would go back to work.

Meanwhile, every night during Passover, little groups of Jesus-followers scurried along the cobblestone streets, darting into simple homes to pray. "Oh, God," they interceded long into the night, "spare our pastor! We're down to the final hours—Herod will strike the first thing Sunday morning—*please do something quick!*" The children no doubt listened, kneeling beside the grown-ups, until their eyes grew heavy and they nodded off to sleep.

Finally came Saturday night, and the prayers grew more desperate. At Mary's home (a sizable one, says tradition, since she was a woman of means), the crowd grew large. They saw no feasible way for Peter to be rescued, but they called out to God nonetheless.

Here in the late twentieth century, how much home praying do *our* children observe? Beyond the perfunctory table graces and bedtime rhymes, do they see and hear us praying on ordinary Tuesdays and Thursdays and Fridays? What about when danger looms—when the house payment is about to be missed, or when someone is sick, or when a relative is threatening divorce? Do we bear down to *pray* at home, or do we simply worry?

Every child needs the shock that Rhoda experienced: "Wow! I can't believe it! We prayed right here in our living room, and it wasn't just a bunch of words—God really heard us! He answered! Wow!"

No wonder, in the next chapter, Mary's son John Mark struck off with Paul and Barnabas on the first missionary journey (Acts 13:5). His life had been touched by an up-close-and-personal encounter with the miracle-working God. He went on, in later years, to write the second Gospel, a power-packed account of Jesus' ministry on earth.

Let us not limit prayer to safe topics ("thank you for this new day") in safe places (church buildings). Right in front of our offsprings' eyes, let us practice exhilarating, faith-stretching prayer.

_____

Lord, I want my kids to know that prayer really
works. I want it to be more than just a ritual.
Increase my faith as I attempt to increase theirs.

DOING THE WORD

Ask yourself: *What major needs, crises, problems am I facing that I haven't voiced in prayer with my children? Why haven't I? Is it because I'm afraid the situation is too complex for God?* (If so, see Gen. 18:14; Jer. 32:17, 27; Matt. 19:26.)

Pick an issue that desperately needs God's intervention. Then, at some *nonstandard* times, take the risk of asking your children to stop and pray with you. Start looking for the answer—and rejoice together when it shows up.

QUESTION TIME

When all the people were safely across, the
Lord said to Joshua,

"Tell the twelve men chosen for a special task, one
from each tribe, each to take a stone from where the
priests are standing in the middle of the Jordan, and to
carry them out and pile them up as a monument at the
place where you camp tonight."

So Joshua summoned the twelve men and told them,
"Go out into the middle of the Jordan where the Ark is.
Each of you is to carry out a stone on your shoulder—
twelve stones in all, one for each of the twelve tribes. We
will use them to build a monument so that in the future,
when your children ask, 'What is this monument for?'
you can tell them, 'It is to remind us that the Jordan
River stopped flowing when the Ark of God went
across!' The monument will be a permanent reminder to
the people of Israel of this amazing miracle."

So the men did as Joshua told them.

That day the entire nation crossed the Jordan River and camped in Gilgal at the eastern edge of the city of Jericho; and there the twelve stones from the Jordan were piled up as a monument.

Then Joshua explained again the purpose of the stones: "In the future," he said, "when your children ask you why these stones are here and what they mean, you are to tell them that these stones are a reminder of this amazing miracle—that the nation of Israel crossed the Jordan River on dry ground! Tell them how the Lord our God dried up the river right before our eyes and then kept it dry until we were all across! It is the same thing the Lord did forty years ago at the Red Sea! He did this so that all the nations of the earth will realize that Jehovah is the mighty God, and so that all of you will worship him forever." (Josh. 4:1-8, 19-24)

The adults were duly impressed. There was the Jordan River frozen in time, the water refusing to obey gravity so a whole nation could cross over. Astounding!

But God knew how short the memory of most people is. How would the next generation, and the next, and the next find out about this mighty miracle? God called for a monument to be erected for the express purpose of getting kids to ask questions.

"What's that, Dad?"

"That pile of boulders?"

"Yeah. How'd they get there?"

"Ah, Son—let me tell you about the incredible day when God stopped this whole river so we could come across—it was fantastic. . . ." And thus the baton of faith would be passed from parent to offspring.

The greatest acts of God can grow dim within twenty years. The hottest revival fires can cool down to sedate embers. It is the task of every adult to introduce the next generation to a God who is active, vigorous, powerful, and even a little overwhelming at times.

How? Well, history lessons are all right, but getting the young person to ask questions is far better. The rock pile served as a teaser; it snagged the curiosity of the child, so that the conversation flowed freely thereafter.

There are dozens of ways, verbal and visual, to do this. Sometimes at bedtime, sometimes in the car, sometimes while fishing or hiking, the teachable moment presents itself. And when it does, seize the opportunity to make the acts of God come alive.

Lord, you've done so many outstanding things for me. Help me to be creative in drawing my children into an encounter with you as well.

DOING THE WORD

Start a notebook in which you record your own personal "Jordan crossings"—instances of God's activity in your life that shouldn't be forgotten. Write down answers to prayer, unexpected blessings, fulfilled promises. Keep adding to the notebook as the years go by. And tell your child the stories as engagingly as possible. Even show the notebook itself if the interest warrants it.

LIVING WITH GOD'S SURPRISES (PART 1)

Zacharias and Elizabeth were godly folk, careful to obey all of God's laws in spirit as well as in letter. But they had no children, for Elizabeth was barren; and now they were both very old.

One day as Zacharias was going about his work in the Temple—for his division was on duty that week—the honor fell to him by lot to enter the inner sanctuary and burn incense before the Lord. Meanwhile, a great crowd stood outside in the Temple court, praying as they always did during that part of the service when the incense was being burned.

Zacharias was in the sanctuary when suddenly an angel appeared, standing to the right of the altar of incense! Zacharias was startled and terrified.

But the angel said, "Don't be afraid, Zacharias! For I have come to tell you that God has heard your prayer, and your wife, Elizabeth, will bear you a son! And you are to name him John. You will both have great joy and gladness at his birth, and many will rejoice with you. For he will be one of the Lord's great men. He must never touch wine or hard liquor—and he will be filled with the Holy Spirit, even from before his birth! And he will persuade many a Jew to turn to the Lord his God. He will be a man of rugged spirit and power like Elijah, the prophet of old; and he will precede the coming of the Messiah, preparing the people for his arrival. He will soften adult hearts to become like little children's, and will change disobedient minds to the wisdom of faith."

Zacharias said to the angel, "But this is impossible! I'm an old man now, and my wife is also well along in years." (Luke 1:6-18)

Well, how would *you* feel if you'd already joined AARP and your wife was finally done with menopause—and then some angel came along talking like this?!

The New Testament era, like the Old Testament era, gets rolling with the account of a very late pregnancy. In each case, God is smilingly sure, while one spouse tries to nod in agreement and the other gasps, "No way!" Back in Genesis, the doubter was the elderly *wife:* Sarai. Here the doubter is the elderly *husband:* Zacharias. Both of them had to get used to God's big surprise.

What this story says to you and me is that God sometimes has rather funny ideas about who is qualified to be a parent. If we had wanted to produce a leader who would rock a nation, calling it to its knees in preparation for the Messiah, we would hardly have chosen this pair.

They lived in the highlands of Judea (see Luke 1:39), away from the cultural and educational advantages of the city.

They obviously would have no other children for John to grow up with, to adjust to, to socialize with. He would be an only child.

And they were simply too *old*. Can you imagine the counsel of a modern OB/GYN: "Now, Elizabeth, you need to understand the high risks of a pregnancy at this age; a fair number of things could go wrong; perhaps you should think about 'alternatives'; if you'd like to consider termination, I can be of assistance. . . ."

Thank God no such "wisdom" was voiced two thousand years ago.

When we are tempted to think the challenge of a new baby (or the child we've already got) is too much, that we can't cope, that God must have selected the wrong house for all this, that "this is impossible!" (v. 18)—it is time to stop and remember Zacharias and Elizabeth. They made it through somehow, and we will too. The end of our story will be more glorious than it looks right now. "God has deliberately chosen to use ideas the world considers foolish and of little worth . . . ," says 1 Corinthians 1:27-29, "so that no one anywhere can ever brag." He knows what he is doing, whether we think so or not.

Lord, you really do take my breath away
sometimes. But if you can take my child and
make him as significant as John the Baptist was,
who am I to object? I'll do my best to
cooperate with your amazing plans.

REFLECTING ON THE WORD

Think back to an earlier surprise in your life, when you were upset and fearful that things wouldn't work out—but they did. Remind yourself of the route by which God brought you this far. Let him know that you will trust him for the present and future, too.

LIVING WITH GOD'S SURPRISES (PART 2)

Zacharias said to the angel, "But this is impossible! I'm an old man now, and my wife is also well along in years."

Then the angel said, "I am Gabriel! I stand in the very presence of God. It was he who sent me to you with this good news! And now, because you haven't believed me, you are to be stricken silent, unable to speak until the child is born. For my words will certainly come true at the proper time."

Meanwhile the crowds outside were waiting for Zacharias to appear and wondered why he was taking so long. When he finally came out, he couldn't speak to them, and they realized from his gestures that he must have seen a vision in the Temple. He stayed on at the Temple for the remaining days of his Temple duties and then returned home. Soon afterwards Elizabeth his wife became pregnant and went into seclusion for five months.

"How kind the Lord is," she exclaimed, "to take away
my disgrace of having no children!" (Luke 1:18-25)

In the face of a divine declaration, Zacharias would have
been better off keeping his mouth shut and just nodding
his head. As it turned out, that's all he got to do for the next
nine months.

He apparently hadn't heard the maxim we teach children
these days about suppertime menus and irascible school-
mates: "If you can't say something good, don't say anything
at all."

Instead, listen to the verbal face-off in the temple:

"I am an old man now. . . ."

"I am Gabriel!"

Are we not prone to pray in the same vein, *informing* God
of how things are here in the *real* world? And he patiently
replies from his far higher point of view.

"Lord, I'm short of money this month for the kids' shoes."

"I am Jehovah-jireh—the God who provides."

"I'm just a housewife."

"I am the one who created and called you."

"I never got to finish college."

"I am the omniscient source of all knowledge."

"I don't like my looks."

"I look not on the outward appearance but on the heart."

"I'm divorced and about to go crazy raising these kids
alone."

"I am a father to the fatherless."

When God sets about to make something happen in our
lives, he will succeed, with or without our endorsement. His

train is moving, picking up speed; it's time to jump on board, as Elizabeth did with her welcoming response (v. 25). To belittle God's idea accomplishes nothing. Far better to echo what God has said, to repeat his promise, to let faith swell in our heart, to foster a spirit of expectancy. After all, what do we have to lose?

God crafts his surprises for our good and for the benefit of his kingdom. If the master planning were left to us, how puny would be the result! The best response to his innovation is to fall in step quickly.

Lord, show me how my life, my home, my family look from your perspective. What potential do you see that I've never noticed? Where might you be taking us? Go ahead and lead; I'll follow.

DOING THE WORD

Try to pray this week about your family without telling God what he already knows. Instead, let him lead the conversation.

LIVING WITH GOD'S SURPRISES (PART 3)

By now Elizabeth's waiting was over, for the time had come for the baby to be born—and it was a boy. The word spread quickly to her neighbors and relatives of how kind the Lord had been to her, and everyone rejoiced.

When the baby was eight days old, all the relatives and friends came for the circumcision ceremony. They all assumed the baby's name would be Zacharias, after his father.

But Elizabeth said, "No! He must be named John!"

"What?" they exclaimed. "There is no one in all your family by that name." So they asked the baby's father, talking to him by gestures.

He motioned for a piece of paper and to everyone's surprise wrote, "His name is *John!*" Instantly Zacharias could speak again, and he began praising God.

Wonder fell upon the whole neighborhood, and the news of what had happened spread through the Judean hills. And everyone who heard about it thought long thoughts and asked, "I wonder what this child will turn out to be? For the hand of the Lord is surely upon him in some special way." (Luke 1:57-66)

Nine months of silence have taught this father a great deal. In his mind he has replayed his quibbling comment to the angel Gabriel a thousand times. Never again will he hesitate in the face of divine direction; he will do what God wants, *pronto.*

But what about the relatives? They swarm around the newborn babe, oohing and gooing, smiling and suggesting. They are solid traditionalists, followers of Cornford's Law: Nothing should ever be done for the first time.

Family advice can often be a wonderful thing, but it is not inerrant. In this case, God had spoken a different word to Zacharias and his wife, and they single-mindedly proceed to shock the aunts and uncles, the sisters and cousins, with a clear statement:

"His name is John."

It is their first step in fulfilling the dream. God immediately flashes his approval by restoring Zacharias's voice. A marvelous prophecy ensues (vv. 67-79), and soon the whole community is talking about what's happening, while any criticism seems to melt away.

What dream is God trying to launch at your house? What bold new venture is he coaxing you to begin? Are you afraid? Would you rather stick with tradition—the way things have always been done by others? Remember, God is not impressed with hesitaters. He wants people who care about what *he* thinks more than what anyone else thinks.

Parenting is more than a matter of common sense. It is a divine calling, and that call often takes on different contours for different parents. Only God, who made your child in the first place, knows what he could do with that special life. Let him name the baby. Let him set the course. Let him chart the future.

---

*Lord, help me discern your voice in the midst of
everybody else's advice. I don't want to be rude,
but neither do I want to be stuck in a rut.
As with John the Baptist, place your hand
upon my child in some special way.*

DOING THE WORD

If you face conflicting advice from relatives that doesn't match God's will for your household, think and pray about how to stay on course without making enemies. What are some peaceful solutions to the situation, some gentle words to say?

AIR POLLUTION

A tree is identified by its fruit. A tree from a select variety produces good fruit; poor varieties don't. You brood of snakes! How could evil men like you speak what is good and right? For a man's heart determines his speech. A good man's speech reveals the rich treasures within him. An evil-hearted man is filled with venom, and his speech reveals it. And I tell you this, that you must give account on Judgment Day for every idle word you speak. (Matt. 12:33-36)

Some people like to make cutting remarks, but the words of the wise soothe and heal. (Prov. 12:18)

Self-control means controlling the tongue! A quick retort can ruin everything. (Prov. 13:3)

Say only what is good and helpful to those you are talking to, and what will give them a blessing. (Eph. 4:29)

S arcasm is a Great American Sport. Foreign visitors to our shores are often amazed at how much of our humor consists of put-downs. While jokes in other cultures often revolve around irony or exaggeration, we are the masters of making another person look foolish.

Television has taught us well to relish the joy of zingers. Our children learn it early, so that family mealtimes and car rides quickly become verbal jousts. The air is regularly befouled. Sure, the punch lines hurt—but they're so witty, so *funny*. And in America, humor is the cultural sugarcoating; we'll swallow just about anything, no matter how toxic, if it makes us laugh.

Wait a minute. Can we really blame all this on the culture, on television, on habit? Jesus said each person's speech comes from an *inner* source. What we say reveals how we think and feel inside. Our words are not really externally driven after all. We honestly don't respect that child, that spouse, that mother-in-law, and so we show it with sarcasm (using a line we heard on some sitcom).

What God is looking for are family members who will *bless* one another instead of bash them—parents who will forgo the thrill of a well-crafted put-down in order to say something positive or (shock!) even complimentary. If that goes against the grain of normal family conversation, so be it. It may not be cool, but it's Christian.

Lord, if you wanted to make wisecracks about me, a less-than-perfect member of your family, you'd have ample opportunity. But you don't.

163

*Thank you for that! And help me to extend the
same charity to the people I live with.*

DOING THE WORD

Next time a family roast is in full swing, filling the air with
acrid fumes, try opening a window. Abruptly change the
subject, or affirm something good that somebody did. See if
you can reroute the conversation.

PICKING UP
THE PIECES

Ahaziah was twenty-two years old when he began to reign, and he reigned one year in Jerusalem. His mother's name was Athaliah, granddaughter of Omri. He, too, walked in the evil ways of Ahab, for his mother encouraged him in doing wrong.

None of his sons, however, except for Joash, lived to succeed him as king, for their grandmother Athaliah killed them when she heard the news of her son Ahaziah's death.

Joash was rescued by his Aunt Jehoshabeath, who was King Ahaziah's sister, and was hidden away in a storage room in the Temple. She was a daughter of King Jehoram and the wife of Jehoiada the priest. Joash remained hidden in the Temple for six years while Athaliah reigned as queen. He was cared for by his nurse and by his aunt and uncle.

In the seventh year of the reign of Queen Athaliah, Jehoiada the priest got up his courage and took some of the army officers into his confidence:

"At last the time has come for the king's son to reign!" Jehoiada exclaimed. "The Lord's promise—that a descendant of King David shall be our king—will be true again."

Joash was seven years old when he became king, and he reigned forty years in Jerusalem. His mother's name was Zibiah, from Beersheba. Joash tried hard to please the Lord all during the lifetime of Jehoiada the priest. (2 Chron. 22:2-3, 9–23:1, 3; 24:1-2)

Trauma is not supposed to happen to infants. Their earliest weeks should be a cocoon of warm love and security. Within the first year of baby Joash's life, his twenty-three-year-old father dies and his grandmother goes on a bloody rampage to kill the rest of the family. She is determined to be undisputed queen of the land, no matter what the cost. Only the quick, desperate bravery of Joash's aunt saves him from the vicious sword.

Did she think in advance what she would *do* with this baby once she snatched him out of harm's way? Probably not. But pausing inside the temple to catch her breath, listening to her pounding heart grow quieter, she found herself facing a new call for her life. In addition to being a priest's wife, she would now need to take up a new service: the ministry of foster parenting.

When a family implodes upon itself, when relatives commit atrocities at home, when facts on the police blotter prove as grisly as tabloid newspaper tales, somebody has to rescue the innocent. Somebody has to surround the petrified child with kindness and peace, repairing the rips in his soul and the gashes in his memory. Somebody has to cling to hope. Somebody has to take a screaming infant and start preparing him to be a king. That is the work of foster moms and dads.

Who would ever have predicted that Joash would one day rule his nation successfully—*for forty years?* The character formation wrought by his aunt and uncle, along with his nurse, made all the difference. A horrendous start was redeemed into a strong adulthood.

In a world of too many broken children, God is still calling men and women to go the extra distance and salvage his little ones.

Lord, would you ever want me to reach out to a needy boy or girl? I think I already have my hands full—but I'm willing at least to listen to your thoughts on the subject.

DOING THE WORD

Make two phone calls to gather information about the needs for foster care in your community—one to a government or private placement agency, the other to a person already doing foster care. Just ask questions and learn some facts, in case you need to know someday.

THAT'S NOT MY JOB!

Jesus knew on the evening of Passover Day that it would be his last night on earth before returning to his Father. During supper the devil had already suggested to Judas Iscariot, Simon's son, that this was the night to carry out his plan to betray Jesus. Jesus knew that the Father had given him everything and that he had come from God and would return to God. And how he loved his disciples! So he got up from the supper table, took off his robe, wrapped a towel around his loins, poured water into a basin, and began to wash the disciples' feet and to wipe them with the towel he had around him.

When he came to Simon Peter, Peter said to him, "Master, you shouldn't be washing our feet like this!"

Jesus replied, "You don't understand now why I am doing it; some day you will."

"No," Peter protested, "you shall never wash my feet!"

"But if I don't, you can't be my partner," Jesus replied.

After washing their feet he put on his robe again and sat down and asked, "Do you understand what I was doing? You call me 'Master' and 'Lord,' and you do well to say it, for it is true. And since I, the Lord and Teacher, have washed your feet, you ought to wash each other's feet. I have given you an example to follow: do as I have done to you. How true it is that a servant is not greater than his master. Nor is the messenger more important than the one who sends him. You know these things—now do them! That is the path of blessing." (John 13:1-8, 12-17)

Does this passage have anything to do with normal family life? After all, it *did* take place in a home.

It is easy to dismiss Jesus' action here as something peculiar to him, something he did on one special occasion just before his death to make a unique point—an unusual, atypical incident.

Except what about his comments in verses 14-17? What is this business about "do as I have done" and "a servant is not greater than his master"?

Footwashing in ancient Palestine was no more fun than it is today. It was a necessary evil. The roads were nothing but dust (with a few horse droppings here and there). Everybody walked. If you wanted a clean house at all, you *had* to remove your sandals and wash your feet upon coming inside. The same held true for your family members and guests.

It didn't take people long to figure out that this was a good job for the household slave to do. Most homes had hired or indentured help, and washing feet was certainly part of their job description.

But when Jesus and the Twelve arrived at the borrowed upper room for their Passover evening, it must have been the slave's day off. Or perhaps footwashing service didn't go with the rental. At any rate, there was no designated foot-washer.

You can bet that the disciples thought of it. James quickly said to himself, *Not me!* Philip concluded, *Not my job.* Andrew thought, *Somebody else will surely volunteer.*

But no one did. The meal began with everyone's feet still dusty.

And then—shock of all shocks!—the Number One Person in the whole room stood up and went to work with a basin and towel. Can you imagine the scene? He kneels down in front of the first speechless disciple; he washes the left foot, dries it, then takes the right foot, dries it . . . then moves his equipment to the second disciple, starting all over. Even Peter gets the treatment, after a little protest.

How long does all this take for a dozen men—fifteen minutes?

Finally, he is finished. Then he poses a searing question: "Do you understand what I was doing?" (v. 12).

Answer: *No. They had not a clue—and in many cases today, neither do we.* We think a leader would cheapen himself by getting his hands dirty. We think no one would respect us if we picked up the slack for a spouse or a child. It would spoil our image.

But was Jesus disrespected for what he did? Quite the opposite. He showed that he was more interested in results than rank, in making the occasion run smoothly than in maintaining his personal prestige. He decided to be part of the solution instead of extending the problem.

His final, tart phrase still penetrates: "You know these things—now do them! That is the path of blessing" (v. 17).

Lord, forgive me for the times I have said
(or thought), "That's not my job—
why doesn't someone else take care of it?"
Keep me from getting too impressed with
myself. Help me look for opportunities
to serve my household, as you did.

DOING THE WORD

The next time a stressful situation comes up at your house, silently ask yourself these two questions:

What do I feel like doing?

What does this situation NEED?

Then ignore your first answer and move into action based on your second answer!

THE MONEY CHASE

Better a little with reverence for God than great treasure and trouble with it.

It is better to eat soup with someone you love than steak with someone you hate. (Prov. 15:16-17)

Dishonest money brings grief to all the family, but hating bribes brings happiness. (Prov. 15:27)

A little gained honestly is better than great wealth gotten by dishonest means. (Prov. 16:8)

Better poor and humble than proud and rich. (Prov. 16:19)

Don't weary yourself trying to get rich. Why waste your time? For riches can disappear as though they had the wings of a bird! (Prov. 23:4-5)

O God, I beg two favors from you before I die: First, help me never to tell a lie. Second, give me neither poverty nor riches! Give me just enough to satisfy my needs! For if I grow rich, I may become content without God. And if I am too poor, I may steal and thus insult God's holy name. (Prov. 30:7-9)

Can a modern family ever have more money than it needs? *Impossible*, we say. There's always a list of purchases waiting, from shoes for the kids to patio furniture to a better stereo system to another car to next year's vacation to . . .

But what does the book of Proverbs say?

It says radical things, like: working class is better than upper class . . . soup is better than steak . . . if you don't have a lot of money, you avoid a lot of temptation and complexity in your life.

It says that certain kinds of money bring grief. It says the money chase can be exhausting, leaving no energy for kids and leisure and laughing and appreciating the nontangibles of life.

J. P. Morgan, a powerful banker and railroad magnate before World War I, was once asked, "How much money would you *like* to earn in a year's time? What would you consider to be enough?"

His eyes slightly crinkled as he replied, "Just a little bit more."

Solomon—a man every bit as wealthy as J. P. Morgan—saw things differently. The scurry for a little bit more is a dead-end street leading not to a mansion but a swamp, he said. It's not worth it. Better to be content with an average standard of living. You don't pay nearly as much in taxes! You're less likely to be robbed: who would want your meager stuff, anyway? You're free to focus on the truly important things, like love and service to others and pleasing God.

Our calling in life is *not* to be a consumer—getting stuff, using it briefly, discarding it, heading out to get some more. In spite of the Great North American Advertising Machine, our true purpose for living is summed up in the little sign that reads, Love People, Use Things. The culture is frantically trying to get us, and our children, to *love things,* and if we have to use people to get the newest things, so be it. That is precisely backwards.

Happiness, says Proverbs, is not in having what you want. It is in wanting what you have.

Lord, I thank you for the fact that I haven't gone hungry recently, I have a roof over my head, I have more than a few things to wear . . . and I have you! Forgive me for being a malcontent sometimes. I honestly don't want the headaches that go along with being wealthy. Teach me to be truly content.

DOING THE WORD

Start a new habit of whispering "Thank you, Lord" when each paycheck or other money comes into your hand. Recognize the Lord's steady provision for your family. Meanwhile, cut down on your catalog browsing and mall cruising. Reduce your fixation on the stuff of modern life.

WHEN NO ONE UNDERSTANDS

[Elkanah] had two wives, Hannah and Peninnah. Peninnah had some children, but Hannah didn't.

Each year Elkanah and his families journeyed to the Tabernacle at Shiloh to worship the Lord of the heavens and to sacrifice to him. (The priests on duty at that time were the two sons of Eli—Hophni and Phinehas.) On the day he presented his sacrifice, Elkanah would celebrate the happy occasion by giving presents to Peninnah and her children; but although he loved Hannah very much, he could give her only one present, for the Lord had sealed her womb; so she had no children to give presents to. Peninnah made matters worse by taunting Hannah because of her barrenness. Every year it was the same—Peninnah scoffing and laughing at her as they went to Shiloh, making her cry so much she couldn't eat.

"What's the matter, Hannah?" Elkanah would exclaim. "Why aren't you eating? Why make such a fuss over having no children? Isn't having me better than having ten sons?"

One evening after supper, when they were at Shiloh, Hannah went over to the Tabernacle. Eli the priest was sitting at his customary place beside the entrance. She was in deep anguish and was crying bitterly as she prayed to the Lord.

And she made this vow: "O Lord of heaven, if you will look down upon my sorrow and answer my prayer and give me a son, then I will give him back to you, and he'll be yours for his entire lifetime, and his hair shall never be cut."

Eli noticed her mouth moving as she was praying silently and, hearing no sound, thought she had been drinking.

"Must you come here drunk?" he demanded. "Throw away your bottle."

"Oh no, sir!" she replied, "I'm not drunk! But I am very sad and I was pouring out my heart to the Lord. Please don't think that I am just some drunken bum!"

"In that case," Eli said, "cheer up! May the Lord of Israel grant you your petition, whatever it is!"

"Oh, thank you, sir!" she exclaimed, and went happily back, and began to take her meals again.

The entire family was up early the next morning and went to the Tabernacle to worship the Lord once more. Then they returned home to Ramah, and when Elkanah slept with Hannah, the Lord remembered her petition; in the process of time, a baby boy was born to her. She

named him Samuel (meaning "asked of God") because,
as she said, "I asked the Lord for him." (1 Sam. 1:2-20)

Sometimes, they just don't get it—"they" being the family
members who live closest to you, who ought to see
what's driving you crazy. The problem is right there in front
of everyone's nose, and yet it seems invisible to all but you.

Part of the stress in Elkanah's house, admittedly, was po-
lygamy. No wonder the human race eventually abandoned
such a prescription for trouble. But those of us who live in
normal marriages still feel some of the same tensions that
ravaged Hannah:

- Infertility when we ache for parenthood
- At least one relative who incessantly (intentionally?)
  says the wrong thing (v. 6)
- Tension that seems to get worse, not better, every time
  we go to worship (have you noticed how marital arguments seem to cluster around Saturdays and Sun-
  days?)
- A husband (or wife) who misses the point altogether.
  In verse 8, Elkanah is wonderfully logical—and miles
  out of touch with his spouse's *emotions*. "C'mon,
  woman—you've got it good. Look on the bright side."
  (Typical male?) Not every family problem submits to
  hardheaded reason.
- Even a minister who misreads the clue (vv. 9-17).
  Sometimes those we expect to be the most helpful, to
  represent God's voice in our lives, can deeply disap-
  point us, even accuse us of sin when we're innocent,

as Eli did. Once the misunderstanding is cleared away, Eli still brushes Hannah off with a cavalier nod to "your petition, whatever it is!"

Yet this sturdy woman clings to hope that at least *God* understands her anguish and will do something about it. Some family tangles can be unknotted only by the Lord, and not all at once. They take time.

When others don't understand, don't even *try* to understand, God is the eternal Comforter, Counselor, and Guide. We are never entirely forsaken.

O Lord, I hope you understand what I'm going through—because a lot of other people don't.
Keep me from lashing back at them,
resenting them, only making matters worse.
Instead, show me how my circumstances
appear to you; give me your perspective.
And lead me toward your resolution.

REINFORCING THE WORD

Choose one of the following Scriptures—the one that best suits your situation—and write it out for a place where you'll see it at least once a day: Psalm 27:10; Psalm 54:4; Psalm 118:6.

HOW TO WRECK
A FAMILY

You may as well know this too, Timothy, that
in the last days it is going to be very difficult to be a
Christian. For people will love only themselves and their
money; they will be proud and boastful, sneering at
God, disobedient to their parents, ungrateful to them,
and thoroughly bad. They will be hardheaded and never
give in to others; they will be constant liars and trouble-
makers and will think nothing of immorality. They will
be rough and cruel, and sneer at those who try to be
good. They will betray their friends; they will be hot-
headed, puffed up with pride, and prefer good times to
worshiping God. They will go to church, yes, but they
won't really believe anything they hear. Don't be taken
in by people like that. (2 Tim. 3:1-5)

I f Paul had been handed a stack of current newsmaga-
zines or a video review of the 1990s, he could not have
written a more accurate description. We are stunned to real-

ize how clearly he seems to be "talking 'bout our generation."

Ten causes of modern family meltdown are here in succinct detail:

- self-centeredness in each family member (v. 2)
- fixation on money (v. 2)
- disobedience to authority (v. 2)
- ungrateful attitude (v. 2)
- tough talk: "it's my way or the highway" (v. 3)
- easy acceptance of things that God says are wrong (v. 3)
- loss of civility and good manners (v. 3)
- disloyalty and impatience (v. 4)
- fun, fun, fun!—that's what counts (v. 4)
- religion with nothing behind the facade (v. 5)

These are the home wreckers, the cultural trends that pull down our stability. They knock the props out from under the place of shelter and goodness that parents and children should be *working together* to build.

Do these ten factors prevail only in homes of busy, crime-ridden metropolitan areas? Are small-town and rural families exempt? No.

Do they thrive only among non-Christians? Are born-again people above all this? Not at all.

We are *all* at risk. Any of us can yield to one, two, or more of the above behaviors without even realizing it. Then the walls and rafters begin to creak under the stress as the support gives way, and we find ourselves in a crisis.

It is our task to be forever vigilant, to swim against the tide of a culture that is not family-friendly, to preserve the love and respect and character that make strong homes. We must stop to take inventory from time to time, reviewing this Scripture and asking ourselves, *Can any of these things be said of us?* The family we save will be our own.

Lord, stiffen me against the adverse winds of my generation. I don't want my family's style to be dictated from the outside. I want us to set our course from your compass, not the culture's. Help me lead the way.

DOING THE WORD

How do you commonly respond when a child or other family member says, "Well, everybody else is doing it," "All my friends at school talk that way," or "Why do we have to be so weird?" Do you hesitate to go against society's grain? Practice your response for the next time such an issue arises.

NO, YOU DON'T

Now the sons of Eli were evil men who didn't love the Lord. It was their regular practice to send out a servant whenever anyone was offering a sacrifice, and while the flesh of the sacrificed animal was boiling, the servant would put a three-pronged fleshhook into the pot and demand that whatever it brought up be given to Eli's sons. They treated all of the Israelites in this way when they came to Shiloh to worship.

So the sin of these young men was very great in the eyes of the Lord; for they treated the people's offerings to the Lord with contempt.

Eli was now very old, but he was aware of what was going on around him. He knew, for instance, that his sons were seducing the young women who assisted at the entrance of the Tabernacle.

"I have been hearing terrible reports from the Lord's people about what you are doing," Eli told his sons. "It is an awful thing to make the Lord's people sin. Ordinary sin receives heavy punishment, but how much more this sin of yours that has been committed against the Lord!" But they wouldn't listen to their father.

One day a prophet came to Eli and gave him this message from the Lord: "Didn't I demonstrate my power when the people of Israel were slaves in Egypt? Didn't I choose your ancestor Levi from among all his brothers to be my priest, and to sacrifice upon my altar, and to burn incense, and to wear a priestly robe as he served me? And didn't I assign the sacrificial offerings to you priests? Then why are you so greedy for all the other offerings which are brought to me? Why have you honored your sons more than me—for you and they have become fat from the best of the offerings of my people!

"Therefore, I, the Lord God of Israel, declare that although I promised that your branch of the tribe of Levi could always be my priests, it is ridiculous to think that what you are doing can continue. I will honor only those who honor me, and I will despise those who despise me. I will put an end to your family, so that it will no longer serve as priests. Every member will die before his time. None shall live to be old. You will envy the prosperity I will give my people, but you and your family will be in distress and need. Not one of them will live out his days. Those who are left alive will live in sadness and grief; and their children shall die by the sword. And to prove that what I have said will come true, I will cause your two sons, Hophni and Phinehas, to die on the same day!"

Then the Lord said to Samuel, "I am going to do a shocking thing in Israel. I am going to do all of the dread-

ful things I warned Eli about. I have continually threat-
ened him and his entire family with punishment because
his sons are blaspheming God, and he doesn't stop
them." (1 Sam. 2:12-14, 17, 22-25, 27-34; 3:11-13)

Headstrong sons (and daughters) have been around for
centuries. And parents—especially high-profile parents, like those in the ministry or other places of leadership—
have been grimacing all the while.

Two things stand out in this sad Scripture:

1. *God holds parents responsible for their children's behavior.*
While Eli's sons are into adulthood—old enough to organize
a shakedown racket that snatched meat from sincere parish-
ioners, old enough to coax various young ladies into bed—
the Lord's heavy rebuke is aimed at their father. Both an
unnamed prophet (chapter 2) and the young Samuel (chapter 3) are sent to Eli with jolting words.

Perhaps God's most telling line of all is in 2:29, "Why have
you honored your sons more than me?" At rock bottom is the
problem that this father is more afraid of his offspring than
he is of the Lord. To crack down on his sons' wrongdoing
would set off an explosion in the house; to let them go on
offending the Lord . . . well, maybe God won't notice.

Wrong. In due time the Lord shows that he is fully awake,
outraged, and set to punish. This story is a powerful statement that God holds fathers responsible for what goes on
under their roof, and he is not impressed with cowardice.

2. *Scolding isn't enough.* Eli bestirs himself enough to lecture
his sons (see 2:23-25), and what he says is quite accurate. But
it falls on deaf ears because it isn't backed up with action.

Talk is cheap. Harangues come easy. Children of all ages wait to find out whether the words will be enforced.

In the end, God tells Samuel that judgment will soon fall on Eli's children because "he doesn't stop them" (3:13). The intentions may have been good, but the results fell short.

There are times in every parent's experience when he or she must say, "You are my child, and since I am answerable to God for you, I will not allow you to do that"—followed by the action it takes to make the words stick. This may cause a furor, but not nearly as much as if God someday has to take matters into his own hands.

Lord, I really don't care for confrontation;
I like peace and tranquillity. Still, give me the
courage to do what I should, to say no with
conviction, to be worthy of the responsibility
you have placed upon my shoulders. May you
never have to step in to punish my children
because I failed to do so. Help us all to realize
that your prohibitions make sense.

DOING THE WORD

While in prayer, ask the Lord to remind you of any correction you've been avoiding with your children, or only moaning and sighing about. If he brings something to mind, summon the courage to take effective action. Let your child know that you have a job to do and that you intend to complete it.

BROTHERLY LOVE
OR
BROTHERLY SHOVE?

For by the grace given me I say to every one of you: Do not think of yourself more highly than you ought, but rather think of yourself with sober judgment, in accordance with the measure of faith God has given you. (Rom. 12:3, NIV)

Don't just pretend that you love others: really love them. Hate what is wrong. Stand on the side of good. Love each other with brotherly affection and take delight in honoring each other. (Rom. 12:9-10)

Who is the most important person in your household? Is it:

The person who brings home the bulk of the money?

The person who does most of the cooking?

The person who does the laundry?

The person with the cheeriest attitude, who lifts everyone else's spirits?

The person who spends the most time in prayer?

A case could be made for any of the above. And in our private moments of reflection (never aloud, of course) we are quite good at it. We frame ourselves as, indeed, the Truly Indispensable Family Member. They really couldn't get along without us!

Paul's dash of cold water on that notion (v. 3) is addressed—did you notice?—*"to every one of you."* Not just the younger children. Not just the cocky teenagers. Not only the wives. The husbands, too. Everybody.

Each of us has a role to play. None of us is the whole stage troupe.

Therefore, we have reason to appreciate each other, which is what verses 9-10 are about. Beyond the perfunctory "I love you," the apostle calls us to genuine affection and enthusiasm about the other family members' worth. No hint here of competition or power struggle. This is a home where each person is the others' biggest fan.

We may retort that Romans 12 is unrealistic; life just doesn't work out that way for us. But wouldn't we *like* to live in such an atmosphere? Wouldn't it be a joy? If we set this ideal before us, could we match up to it for one evening? What about a full day? Then maybe a whole weekend?

If we think a lifestyle of personal modesty and focusing on others is impossible, of course it will be. If we think that God just might help us make our home a delight instead of a headache, we may be in for a pleasant surprise.

Lord, I can't speak for the other people under my roof—but I can speak for myself. I want to live and act the way these Scriptures describe.

Cleanse me of self-promotion. Give me genuine
love for those who sometimes irritate me.
Make this home a haven, starting with me.

DOING THE WORD

On a piece of paper, write each family member's name and two reasons to think highly of him or her. What are two character traits that you can honor? Then find a time in the next forty-eight hours to verbalize one or both of those items to the individual: "You know what? It's really special the way you . . ."

FORWARD PASS

O my people, listen to my teaching. Open
your ears to what I am saying. For I will show you lessons from our history, stories handed down to us from
former generations. I will reveal these truths to you so
that you can describe these glorious deeds of Jehovah to
your children and tell them about the mighty miracles
he did. For he gave his laws to Israel and commanded
our fathers to teach them to their children, so that they in
turn could teach their children too. Thus his laws pass
down from generation to generation. In this way each
generation has been able to obey his laws and to set its
hope anew on God and not forget his glorious miracles.
Thus they did not need to be as their fathers were—stubborn, rebellious, unfaithful, refusing to give their hearts
to God. (Ps. 78:1-8)

Two things stand out in this passage:
  1. *For the next generation of kids to turn out godly, parents*

must play a verbal role. Parents have lived long enough to know what consequences are all about. They can tell the stories of how Grandma's faith kept the family together during hard times, or how God answered prayer when Dad desperately needed a job.

We parents are *key interpreters* of life to our children. We must not leave the task of spiritual input to "the experts"—ministers, youth workers, Sunday school teachers, et al. We must be more than silent taxi drivers who haul our kids to others for instruction. A big part of the action is *ours.*

In fact, William Barclay, the noted Scottish theologian, wrote in his book *Train Up a Child,* "The New Testament knows nothing about religious education and nothing about schools, for the New Testament is certain that the only training which really matters is given within the home, and that there are no teachers so effective for good or evil as parents are."

2. *Part of the message we pass along to kids is "Don't repeat our mistakes! Don't mess up the way our generation did!"* That's awfully candid, and maybe a little hard on our adult image—but isn't that what verse 8 says? God bluntly assigns us to hang out the dirty laundry so kids can learn how to live clean. Be honest enough to tell (at the appropriate time) of a mistake you made in the past and the pain and suffering that resulted—for you and for others. Show the results of bad choices. After all, the Scriptures do this in living color.

To paraphrase Santayana, the child who learns not from history is destined to repeat it.

Lord, I will pass along the lessons of the
past—both good and bad. Help my children

to absorb them and serve you
more faithfully as a result.

DOING THE WORD

Think of the most positive story you could share with your children about their forebears' walk with God. Then think about the most poignant warning story. Be looking for teachable moments—in the car, at bedtime, after a leisurely meal at home or in a restaurant—to tell both of these stories.

When the Truth Hurts

Where is that happy spirit that we felt together then? For in those days I know you would gladly have taken out your own eyes and given them to replace mine if that would have helped me.

And now have I become your enemy because I tell you the truth? (Gal. 4:15-16)

If we say that we have no sin, we are only fooling ourselves and refusing to accept the truth. But if we confess our sins to him, he can be depended on to forgive us and to cleanse us from every wrong. [And it is perfectly proper for God to do this for us because Christ died to wash away our sins.] If we claim we have not sinned, we are lying and calling God a liar, *for he says we have sinned*. (1 John 1:8-10)

Couples joke about how starry-eyed they were in the beginning days, how blissfully blind was young love.

And then they discovered the truth of the T-shirt sold in the tourist shops: "Pobody's nerfect."

It's more than just leaving dirty socks on the bedroom floor or neglecting to bring home the charge card receipts. Those things are passed over easily enough. But what do you do when you're truly disappointed in your spouse, when the issue is significant (at least to you), and the more you try to talk about it, the more you seem like an "enemy" (v. 16) instead of a loving partner?

Everyone says about marriage, "You have to work at it." But what if your work seems only to aggravate the situation?

Elisabeth Elliot once wrote to her daughter:

> Who is it you marry? You marry a sinner. There's nobody else to marry. That ought to be obvious enough, but when you love a man as you love yours it's easy to forget. You forget it for a while, and then when something happens that ought to remind you, you find yourself wondering what's the matter, how could this happen, where did things go wrong? They went wrong back in the Garden of Eden. Settle it once for all, your husband is a son of Adam. Acceptance of him—of all of him—includes acceptance of his being a sinner. He is a fallen creature in need of the same kind of redemption all the rest of us are in need of, and liable to all the temptations which are "common to man."
>
> You will find yourself disarmed utterly, and your accusing spirit transformed into loving forgiveness the moment you remember that you did, in fact, marry only a sinner, and *so did he.*

It does no good to pretend otherwise, says the apostle John; "we are only fooling ourselves" (v. 8). But it does a great deal of good to confess our sins, to clear the air both with God and with our spouse. Whether our candor and honesty bring forth a reciprocal confession from the other side is not really the point. We can walk with fresh eyes and a clean heart because we have named the fact that we sinned.

The truth that hurts, hurts either way. If buried and brushed over, it goes on hurting, like a dull ache in the relationship. If brought to the surface and confronted, it stings for the moment, but then it evaporates in the warmth of resolution. Like a splinter being pulled from a fingertip, we can touch the spot with relief, knowing that healing can now begin.

O Lord, you know every one of my shortcomings—and so does my spouse. So why do I play cover-up games? Give me the courage to face hard facts without flinching, so that our relationship can be strengthened.

DOING THE WORD

In your mind, try to put yourself in your spouse's shoes for a minute. What foible, what failing of yours would he or she most like to get cleared up? Instead of waiting to be cornered on this topic, go ahead and take the initiative. Find the right time to say, "You know, I'm sure I drive you crazy with my _____. I'm genuinely sorry about that, and I'd like you to forgive me. Here's how I intend to change. . . ." Then pray together about this difficulty.

R-Rated
Rationales

In his old age King David was confined to his bed; but no matter how many blankets were heaped upon him, he was always cold.

"The cure for this," his aides told him, "is to find a young virgin to be your concubine and nurse. She will lie in your arms and keep you warm."

So they searched the country from one end to the other to find the most beautiful girl in all the land. Abishag, from Shunam, was finally selected. They brought her to the king, and she lay in his arms to warm him (but he had no sexual relations with her).

Then David died and was buried in Jerusalem. He had reigned over Israel for forty years, seven of them in Hebron and thirty-three in Jerusalem. And Solomon became the new king, replacing his father David; and his kingdom prospered.

One day Adonijah, the son of Haggith, came to see Solomon's mother, Bathsheba.

"Have you come to make trouble?" she asked him.

"No," he replied, "I come in peace. As a matter of fact, I have a favor to ask of you."

"What is it?" she asked.

"Everything was going well for me," he said, "and the kingdom was mine: everyone expected me to be the next king. But the tables are turned, and everything went to my brother instead; for that is the way the Lord wanted it. But now I have just a small favor to ask of you; please don't turn me down."

"What is it?" she asked.

He replied, "Speak to King Solomon on my behalf (for I know he will do anything you request) and ask him to give me Abishag, the Shunammite, as my wife."

"All right," Bathsheba replied, "I'll ask him."

So she went to ask the favor of King Solomon. The king stood up from his throne as she entered and bowed low to her. He ordered that a throne for his mother be placed beside his; so she sat at his right hand.

"I have one small request to make of you," she said. "I hope you won't turn me down."

"What is it, my mother?" he asked. "You know I won't refuse you."

"Then let your brother Adonijah marry Abishag," she replied.

"Are you crazy?" he demanded. "If I were to give him Abishag, I would be giving him the kingdom too! For he is my older brother! He and Abiathar the priest and General Joab would take over!" Then King Solomon swore with a great oath, "May God strike me dead if Adonijah does not die this very day for this plot against me! I swear it by the living God who has given me the throne of my father David and this kingdom he promised me."

So King Solomon sent Benaiah to execute him, and he killed him with a sword. (1 Kings 1:1-4; 2:10-25)

What a strange story! You've probably never heard a sermon on *this* text. (Half the congregation would be blushing.)

But there's a lesson here for married people in their mid-to-later years. David is not as strong and virile as he used to be; in fact, his health is slipping fast. His sluggish circulation is causing hypothermia. Somebody needs to warm him up.

We may naturally ask, Why not his wife?! In fact, he has several to choose from. Isn't that part of marital commitment, "in sickness and in health, till death do us part"?

No, the palace staff has a different idea. They go hunting for a gorgeous young thing with creamy skin and stunning figure to come raise the king's temperature, while they no doubt stand around the hallways making risqué jokes. . . .

What does Abishag think of all this? Is she embarrassed? Does she hate every minute? The Scripture doesn't say.

Regardless, the point for us is this: *Beware of schemes and rationalizations about "somebody else" who can meet my particular need of the moment.* A listening ear, a quick mind, a witty tongue—qualities lacking in a spouse but available just for the time being in this other person . . .

Down that road lies trouble.

The rest of the story shows that in such cases, *the plot always thickens.* The easy friendship leads to complications. It so happened that two of David's sons were in a fierce battle for the throne. Adonijah was losing, Solomon was winning—and Abishag became a pawn in Adonijah's scheme to pull out a last-minute comeback. If he could just marry her, his claim to his father's legacy would take a jump.

Solomon saw right through this scheme and had him summarily executed. Abishag no doubt went home wondering how to erase the past few weeks and start life all over.

In marital hanky-panky, even without actual sex, somebody always gets hurt—and not necessarily the original perpetrator. What seems so innocent and fail-safe at the beginning has a way of unraveling. God's plan for *one* man and *one* woman to face life's trials together, exclusively, is still the best.

Lord, whenever my imagination starts focusing
on my "needs" rather than your holiness—
slap me fast.

REMEMBERING THE WORD

Write this down and put it in a private location where you will still see it (a clothing drawer, on the back wall of your closet):

Husbands: "In case anyone asks, I am a one-woman man."

Wives: "In case anyone asks, I am a one-man woman."

How Much Help Is Too Much?

> Brothers, if someone is caught in a sin, you
> who are spiritual should restore him gently. But watch
> yourself, or you also may be tempted. Carry each other's
> burdens, and in this way you will fulfill the law of
> Christ. If anyone thinks he is something when he is noth-
> ing, he deceives himself. Each one should test his own
> actions. Then he can take pride in himself, without com-
> paring himself to somebody else, for each one should
> carry his own load. (Gal. 6:1-5, NIV)

There's a definite tension in this passage over the issue of
self-reliance.

Verse 2 has a nice, soft, gentle touch to it: "Carry each
other's burdens, and in this way you will fulfill the law of
Christ." We can almost hear in the background the mellow
strains of the old Beatles song "I get by with a little help from
my friends."

Then what is the apostle saying in verses 4-5? Suddenly the

edge turns hard: "Each one should test his own actions . . . take pride in himself . . . carry his own load."

Which is it, Paul?

We need to know, because this matter comes up all the time in family life. "Mom, I'm running late this morning; can you make my bed for me?" "How come Shelly won't help me with my homework?" "Dear, if you could just give Michael his bath tonight . . ."

How far are we all expected to go in picking up the other person's responsibilities? When does helpfulness cross the line into supporting somebody's laziness? What is normal give-and-take, and what is manipulation? If I say yes to this request, will I be showing Christian kindness, or will I simply be a sucker?

Parents face it. Siblings face it. Spouses face it. Naturally, we all want to live by verse 2 when *we* need help and enforce verse 5 when others do!

The solution to this dilemma lies in understanding that verse 5 ("carry your own load") is the Standard Operating Procedure, the norm for daily practice. Meanwhile, verse 2 ("carry each other's burdens") is the back-up plan. Verse 2 goes into action when the person *can't* perform verse 5. If the person is "caught in a sin" (v. 1), if the person is ill or stressed or in any way struggling, of course it is the Christian way to help him or her, to come alongside and pick up the load. But under normal conditions, self-reliance and responsibility should be the order of the day.

Many of us, if we are not careful, tilt to one side or the other. The balance of this Scripture is not always easy to live out. But with practice, we can manage to run our households in an organized *and* compassionate manner.

Lord, save me from hypocrisy in this area, from demanding more from others than I am willing to give myself. Teach me more of what it means to "fulfill the law of Christ" in my home.

DOING THE WORD

Think back to the last time you felt taken advantage of by a family member. What were the circumstances? Was it indeed a time for bearing the other's burden or for insisting on self-reliance? Did you go ahead and help—but with a sour attitude? What would you do differently next time? Think about the requests that seem to come repeatedly, and set your plan of response in advance.

At Wits' End

So the people of Israel continued to multiply
and to become a mighty nation.

Then Pharaoh commanded all of his people to throw
the newborn Hebrew boys into the Nile River. But the
girls, he said, could live.

There were at this time a Hebrew fellow and girl of the
tribe of Levi who married and had a family, and a baby
son was born to them. When the baby's mother saw that
he was an unusually beautiful baby, she hid him at
home for three months. Then, when she could no longer
hide him, she made a little boat from papyrus reeds, wa-
terproofed it with tar, put the baby in it, and laid it
among the reeds along the river's edge. The baby's sister
watched from a distance to see what would happen to
him.

Well, this is what happened: A princess, one of Pharaoh's daughters, came down to bathe in the river, and
as she and her maids were walking along the riverbank,

she spied the little boat among the reeds and sent one of the maids to bring it to her. When she opened it, there was a baby! And he was crying. This touched her heart. "He must be one of the Hebrew children!" she said.

Then the baby's sister approached the princess and asked her, "Shall I go and find one of the Hebrew women to nurse the baby for you?"

"Yes, do!" the princess replied. So the little girl rushed home and called her mother!

"Take this child home and nurse him for me," the princess instructed the baby's mother, "and I will pay you well!" So she took him home and nursed him.

Later, when he was older, she brought him back to the princess and he became her son. She named him Moses (meaning "to draw out") because she had drawn him out of the water. (Exod. 1:20–2:10)

This is *not* a sweet little Sunday school story. This is dreadful; a nation is being murdered. A systematic genocide is underway, an ancient holocaust as heinous as anything Hitler would devise. At least his gas ovens would leave a trail of smoke and ash; the Hebrew babies sank into the Nile without a trace.

In the midst of this terror, Jochebed discovers she is pregnant for the third time. Imagine her nightly prayer: "O Lord Jehovah, please, *please* let it be a girl." She prays as the months pass along to escape Pharaoh's vile decree, and finally comes labor and delivery . . . and it is not a girl.

The infant sleeps a lot at first, like any newborn. But the weeks pass, and little Moses grows inevitably more noisy.

What if they are discovered? The whole family is now at risk. Jochebed has managed as long as she can—*but something has to give.*

Should she kill her son? No. Finally, she decides to obey Pharaoh. She will put her son into the river as ordered. *But the law didn't say anything about flotation devices!* She preserves his safety just a bit longer, knowing full well that within hours he will die anyway of heat, of dehydration, or by becoming fussy and capsizing the basket.

She gives him up to God's mercy. And after all human effort is exhausted, *then comes the miracle.* The princess shows up . . . her heart is touched . . . and before the day is over, God has done exceedingly abundantly above what Jochebed could ever have asked or thought. Her son's life is spared, and he's back in his own godly home to be raised—at government expense!

God is a God of many options. When our children's future seems doomed, when our heart is being ripped into nineteen pieces, when we've run out of bright ideas—he often steps in with an astounding reversal. We stand with our mouths hanging open as he takes action, a broad smile on his face.

No wonder the psalmist wrote that his mercy endures *forever.*

O Lord, next time I'm frantic and desperate,
I'll be looking for your last-minute intervention.
My heart will be pounding,
but in my head I will know that
you always have my needs in view.

REINFORCING THE WORD

Find a hymnal and read aloud (or sing) all the stanzas of "Children of the Heavenly Father" or "God Will Take Care of You."

WHEN PRIORITIES CLASH

Some Pharisees and other Jewish leaders now arrived from Jerusalem to interview Jesus.

"Why do your disciples disobey the ancient Jewish traditions?" they demanded. "For they ignore our ritual of ceremonial handwashing before they eat." He replied, "And why do your traditions violate the direct commandments of God? For instance, God's law is 'Honor your father and mother; anyone who reviles his parents must die.' But you say, 'Even if your parents are in need, you may give their support money to the church instead.' And so, by your man-made rule, you nullify the direct command of God to honor and care for your parents. You hypocrites! Well did Isaiah prophesy of you, 'These people say they honor me, but their hearts are far away. Their worship is worthless, for they teach their man-made laws instead of those from God.'" (Matt. 15:1-9)

The church should take loving care of women whose husbands have died if they don't have anyone else to help them. But if they have children or grandchildren, these are the ones who should take the responsibility, for kindness should begin at home, supporting needy parents. This is something that pleases God very much.

Anyone who won't care for his own relatives when they need help, especially those living in his own family, has no right to say he is a Christian. Such a person is worse than the heathen. (1 Tim. 5:3-4, 8)

In a day of Social Security, pension funds, and IRA accounts, do these Scriptures have any relevance? Can we just skip these sections, assuming our parents are well-heeled for their sunset years?

Not necessarily.

It is true that Jesus and Paul spoke in a culture without government safety nets; if the elderly hadn't amassed enough assets to see them through, they were at the mercy of their children and the almsgiving public. Thus Paul called upon the church to get organized and give stipends to widows who *didn't* have nearby family.

But here in modern times, what about the other needs of elderly parents? What about providing companionship and a sense of worth, or even helping with household repairs that require an agility they no longer possess? All these are ways to "honor your father and mother."

The underlying point of these passages is as valid today as in the first century: *Beware of rationalizing. Beware of assuming that your senior relatives will somehow, some way fend for them-*

selves *without too much of your involvement. Don't get so spiritually minded that you're no family good.*

Whether it's an elderly mother with a plumbing problem, a fourth grader with a Little League game on the same night as a church committee meeting, or a spouse simply needing to talk, the Christian faith is intrinsically pro-family, pro-relationship. God is not impressed with those who tap-dance away from such priorities. Jesus called them hypocrites. Paul said they were "worse than the heathen." Strong reprimands from two *single* men who might be expected to promote their own life's love—the kingdom of God, the church—over all other competition. Not so.

Traditions and habits—even respectable ones—must never come before the needs of those whom we say we love the most.

---

*Lord, guide me in honoring my parents (and
parents-in-law), even now that I'm an adult.
Show me ways I'm not giving to them, and to
the rest of my family, what you want me to give.
Let me never build in any of them
a resentment of you because of what
I do or don't do on their behalf.*

DOING THE WORD

Stop and think for five minutes about your parents and in-laws. What do they need? How could you show them more honor? How could Jesus be more real to them through your actions?

THE FAVORED
CHILD

Jacob's son Joseph was now seventeen years
old. His job, along with his half-brothers, the sons of his
father's wives Bilhah and Zilpah, was to shepherd his
father's flocks. But Joseph reported to his father some of
the bad things they were doing. Now as it happened,
Israel loved Joseph more than any of his other children,
because Joseph was born to him in his old age. So one
day Jacob gave him a special gift—a brightly colored
coat. His brothers of course noticed their father's partial-
ity, and consequently hated Joseph; they couldn't say a
kind word to him. One night Joseph had a dream and
promptly reported the details to his brothers, causing
even deeper hatred.

"Listen to this," he proudly announced. "We were out
in the field binding sheaves, and my sheaf stood up, and
your sheaves all gathered around it and bowed low before it!"

"So you want to be our king, do you?" his brothers derided. And they hated him both for the dream and for his cocky attitude.

Then he had another dream and told it to his brothers. "Listen to my latest dream," he boasted. "The sun, moon, and eleven stars bowed low before me!" This time he told his father as well as his brothers; but his father rebuked him. "What is this?" he asked. "Shall I indeed, and your mother and brothers come and bow before you?" His brothers were fit to be tied concerning this affair, but his father gave it quite a bit of thought and wondered what it all meant. (Gen. 37:2-11)

Some children are just a lot more fun than others. From early days they make us smile; they do what we ask; they easily see things our way. Their middle name should be Delight.

We know in our head that we should treat all our offspring equally. But down in our heart, it's a different story. We end up repeating Jacob's mistake, giving the favored child some form of colorful coat (perhaps invisible but nonetheless real)—an extra quota of smiles, the benefit of the doubt, a compliment or gentle touch to the shoulder. And the siblings watch in smoldering silence.

Well, didn't the kid *deserve* it? After all, he earned that A. He worked hard. He followed instructions without back talk.

If we could raise children one at a time, parenting would be a lot simpler. (But of course, who'd have the energy at sixty and seventy?!) The combination of several very different sons and daughters under one roof calls for maximum wisdom.

Young Joseph, knowing he was unique among the siblings, felt free to share his self-aggrandizing dreams. Would he have boasted so if his father had not already set him up as special? Perhaps not. After the second dream, even Jacob tried to get his son to forgo his promenading, but the damage was already done; the older brothers were "fit to be tied" (v. 11).

In the end of this chapter, they tied the hateful coat into a bloody heap and threw it at their father's feet, plunging him into more than a decade of grief and depression. God eventually brought good out of this family's malfunction—but that did not excuse Jacob's ineptness in the early days. He owed it to each of his children, including the biggest pain in the neck, to guide with a skillful combination of love and discipline, "for God treats everyone the same" (Rom. 2:11).

Lord, I don't know why you gave my children the combination of personality types and temperaments you did—but I accept each of them as your special gift. May no one in this house feel less loved than someone else. May I bring each one to the very best you have in mind for him or her.

APPLYING THE WORD

Be brutally honest as you ask yourself, *Do I have a favorite child?* Give the real answer, not the "correct" answer. Then think through each of your offspring and name two or three things you can applaud, appreciate, affirm. Make a vow to spread the praise evenly in your home.

"CRUNCH, CHOMP, GOBBLE"

> For you were called to freedom, brethren;
> only do not use your freedom as an opportunity for the
> flesh, but through love be servants of one another. For
> the whole law is fulfilled in one word, "You shall love
> your neighbor as yourself." But if you bite and devour
> one another take heed that you are not consumed by one
> another. (Gal. 5:13-15, RSV)

Freedom is a wonderful, dreadful thing. It lets us say and do whatever we like! And therein lies the risk.

A home that stands for "free speech" can be a dangerous place. As verse 15 says, one biting comment leads to another. *Snap, nibble, crunch, chomp, gobble, gobble*—and before you know it, there's nothing left. Two people's fragile egos are reduced to a pile of masticated bones and flesh.

According to Mother Goose:

There once were two cats of Kilkenny.
    Each thought there was one cat too many;

So they fought and they fit,
　　And they scratched and they bit,
Till, excepting their nails,
　　And the tips of their tails,
Instead of two cats, there weren't any.

In the same way, family members can consume one another if they're not careful.

How much better to remember the immortal words of Benjamin Franklin to his colleagues as they signed the Declaration of Independence that hot July afternoon: "We must all hang together, or assuredly we shall all hang separately." In other words, their choices were to unify and stand by one another, or suffer certain defeat at British hands.

Marriages are equally vulnerable. Households face a multitude of foes. And this Scripture teaches us that we can do so many *good* things with our freedom. We can choose to serve each other. We can voluntarily help a child with homework, make a bed for someone, surprise someone with a compliment, give an unrequested backrub . . . why? Because we love them.

The second great commandment says to love our neighbor as ourselves. Who is a closer neighbor than the person who shares our bed or sleeps in the bedroom down the hall? The place to start loving is at ground zero, in our own homes. Then we can spread out in concentric circles to the wider world.

This is not freedom by modern assumptions, i.e., the freedom to speak as bluntly and coarsely as I wish, to insult, to slack off, to do whatever makes me feel good, to make a mess, to center on my own urges. All that is merely what Paul meant in verse 13 by "an opportunity for the flesh."

Instead, we can put freedom to higher, nobler uses, in building a home that honors God and strengthens its members. That is freedom indeed.

Lord, it sounds strange—"free to serve."
But I accept this role, understanding that it
means freedom from having to promote myself,
to defend my interests, to stand guard over my
personal castle. Instead, you have set me free to
give, to support, to build up my "neighbors"
under my own roof. Keep reminding
me of this, Lord. I need it!

REINFORCING THE WORD

Write out Galatians 5:15 and post it on the refrigerator for two weeks.

PAYING THE BILLS

It is better to have little and be godly than to own an evil man's wealth; for the strength of evil men shall be broken, but the Lord takes care of those he has forgiven.

Day by day the Lord observes the good deeds done by godly men, and gives them eternal rewards. He cares for them when times are hard; even in famine, they will have enough. But evil men shall perish. These enemies of God will wither like grass and disappear like smoke. Evil men borrow and "cannot pay it back"! But the good man returns what he owes with some extra besides. Those blessed by the Lord shall inherit the earth, but those cursed by him shall die.

The steps of good men are directed by the Lord. He delights in each step they take. If they fall it isn't fatal, for the Lord holds them with his hand.

I have been young and now I am old. And in all my years I have never seen the Lord forsake a man who loves him; nor have I seen the children of the godly go hungry. Instead, the godly are able to be generous with their gifts and loans to others, and their children are a blessing. (Ps. 37:16-26)

Parenting, among other things, is *an act of financial faith.* If you were plotting your next twenty years with an eye to accumulate as much money as possible, you would never have kids. Kids are expensive—at least $100,000 apiece by the time you get them launched into adulthood and paying their own way. So if you take up the task of raising one or more children in North America today, you need the above psalm!

Many of us have grown a shade jealous looking at our childless, two-salary neighbors. We think about it: No trips to the pediatrician. No baby-sitter fees. No weekly allowances. No need to own a van. No call for an additional bedroom or two. No orthodontics. No sudden jump in car insurance rates when kids reach sixteen. Most of all, no college tuition, room, board, or books. Meanwhile, lots of quiet, affordable dinners for two, at which the main topic of discussion is planning the next vacation to Hawaii. . . .

But God called us to be *parents.* And his call includes the promises that he will care for us "when times are hard" (v. 19); that he will guide our steps (v. 23); that throughout the years, our children will not go hungry (v. 25). In fact, there's nothing wrong with being godly and having little, says verse 16. It beats quite a number of alternatives.

When shaken by the mounting bills, when discouraged to see no progress in the savings account, when frightened at the thought of college bills ahead, remember the words of the hymn: "Great is thy faithfulness . . . *all I have needed thy hand hath provided.*" And affirm, with David, that children are indeed a blessing in ways no banker can tally.

Lord, somehow provide the means for me to complete this assignment. My hope, my trust, is not in my employer but in you.

DOING THE WORD

Next payday, when you sit down to pay your bills, stop and read this psalm first. Thank the Lord for the money you *do* have rather than grouse about the amount you don't. Then proceed to write your checks with a calm spirit.

ENOUGH ALREADY

Paul writes to the Philippian church:

> How grateful I am and how I praise the Lord
> that you are helping me again. I know you have always
> been anxious to send what you could, but for a while
> you didn't have the chance. Not that I was ever in need,
> for I have learned how to get along happily whether I
> have much or little. I know how to live on almost noth-
> ing or with everything. I have learned the secret of con-
> tentment in every situation, whether it be a full stomach
> or hunger, plenty or want; for I can do everything God
> asks me to with the help of Christ who gives me the
> strength and power.
>
> And it is he who will supply all your needs from his
> riches in glory because of what Christ Jesus has done for
> us. (Phil. 4:10-13, 19)

Is anyone content these days? In a world dripping with
ads and commercials, luring us round the clock to-

ward newer, better, shinier cars, shoes, video games, and vacations . . . isn't it chronic to want more, more, more?

At the time Paul wrote these verses, he had lost it all. He was down to the meager existence of a Roman jail . . . maybe that's what lies behind his statement "I *have learned the secret* of contentment in every situation" (v. 12, emphasis added).

This passage most definitely does not fit the North American ethos. We *deserve* the best (so say the ads); we've got it coming to us; our expectations have been jacked to ever-higher levels. And if we don't get the things we think we deserve, then life is really a bummer, isn't it?

Paul was not keyed to *accumulation.* He wasn't turned on by the thought of more and more appliances, experiences, trips, and assets. His goal was *contentment.*

If our children are to think this way, we will have *to teach them* to be satisfied, whether they wear designer jeans or a cousin's hand-me-downs, whether they get to enjoy an amusement park or stay home and play Monopoly, whether they have money for McDonald's or carry a sack lunch. How?

By being content ourselves. By debunking the propaganda of a materialistic society. By poking fun at overblown commercials. By clearly distinguishing between true needs and mere wants. By affirming to young and old alike that we "can do everything through him who gives [us] strength."

Verse 13 has long been cherished by many Christians as a pep phrase. "Through Christ I can get this next promotion . . . I can lose fifteen pounds and look great . . . I can get an A in this night course I'm taking. . . ." Whatever the merits of those pursuits, let us not skip past what Paul was talking about: being content *regardless* of the circumstances. Whether in a bull market or a bear market. Whether riding high among his fellow apostles or locked up in a Roman dungeon.

God has promised (v. 19) to meet all our *needs*—not necessarily our wants, our fantasies, our wishes, especially as fanned by modern magazines and catalogs and TV shows, but still, our "needs." And for that, we can be sincerely grateful.

Lord, make this home an island of contentment
in a feverish consumer world . . .
starting with me.

DOING THE WORD

- Listen to your own language; how often do you say "I need" when what you really mean is "I want"? Revise your sentences for more accuracy.
- Debunk a handful of commercials tonight on television. Talk with your family about which items are essential and which are luxuries.

RENT A WOMB?

Sarai and Abram had no children. So Sarai took her maid, an Egyptian girl named Hagar, and gave her to Abram to be his second wife.

"Since the Lord has given me no children," Sarai said, "you may sleep with my servant girl, and her children shall be mine."

And Abram agreed. (This took place ten years after Abram had first arrived in the land of Canaan.) So he slept with Hagar, and she conceived; and when she realized she was pregnant, she became very proud and arrogant toward her mistress Sarai.

Then Sarai said to Abram, "It's all your fault. For now this servant girl of mine despises me, though I myself gave her the privilege of being your wife. May the Lord judge you for doing this to me!"

"You have my permission to punish the girl as you see fit," Abram replied. So Sarai beat her and she ran away. (Gen. 16:1-6)

The notion of surrogate motherhood is not nearly so modern as we think. Here, almost four thousand years ago, an infertile husband and wife come up with a desperate scheme to end their years of frustration: *Let's get somebody else to bear our child.*

What they failed to predict was the emotional fallout of such an arrangement. Procreation is much more than biological. It touches the deepest feelings not only of women but of men as well.

Before the nine months of pregnancy are even complete, all chaos has broken loose. A caldron of unforeseen stresses and complications has come to the surface. Hagar is no longer the humble, quiet charwoman; she flaunts her new status. Sarai is furious, so furious she cannot think straight enough to remember who concocted this idea in the first place. She accuses her husband of alienating the whole household. Abram throws up his hands in exasperation. Harsh words fly, and soon Hagar moves out, taking her one bargaining chip (her developing baby in the womb) with her.

Marriage and childbearing are part of the divine order, and it seldom pays to tinker with the dynamics. While science has found amazing ways to help some couples achieve their dreams, it has also opened up new dilemmas. Children must be nurtured in a climate of trust and commitment, from start to finish, and the role of mother and father did not come about by chance.

Thank you, Lord, for conceiving this
very special job called parent.

Think about the ways in which bearing children is a divine calling, not just a biological process. How does this affect your view of pregnancy? How does it relate to day-to-day parenting?

"LORD, IN CASE YOU'VE FORGOTTEN—"

Then, teaching them more about prayer, he used this illustration: "Suppose you went to a friend's house at midnight, wanting to borrow three loaves of bread. You would shout up to him, 'A friend of mine has just arrived for a visit and I've nothing to give him to eat.' He would call down from his bedroom, 'Please don't ask me to get up. The door is locked for the night and we are all in bed. I just can't help you this time.'

"But I'll tell you this—though he won't do it as a friend, if you keep knocking long enough, he will get up and give you everything you want—just because of your persistence. And so it is with prayer—keep on asking and you will keep on getting; keep on looking and you will keep on finding; knock and the door will be opened. Everyone who asks, receives; all who seek, find; and the door is opened to everyone who knocks.

"You men who are fathers—if your boy asks for bread, do you give him a stone? If he asks for fish, do you give him a snake? If he asks for an egg, do you give him a scorpion? [Of course not!]

"And if even sinful persons like yourselves give children what they need, don't you realize that your heavenly Father will do at least as much, and give the Holy Spirit to those who ask for him?" (Luke 11:5-13)

This story has always been troubling, because it makes God seem reluctant, surly, tightfisted, a bit of a grouch. (Of course, if someone rang *our* telephone in the middle of the night and woke up our kids, we wouldn't be exactly charming, either.)

Perhaps the scene is better understood by focusing on the pesky neighbor. He *is* rather high-strung, don't you think? So his best buddy from Buffalo has just dropped in on him unexpectedly—do they *have* to have a midnight snack? Is his own cupboard *totally* bare? Not even a bag of pretzels or a Pepsi?

If so, how about just going on to bed and finding some food in the morning? Why does he have to have three loaves of bread *right now?*

When seen in this light, we can start to appreciate Jesus' point that *even oddball and unlikely requests are all right to bring the Father.* He may, like the man in the story, let out a deep sigh and scratch his head—but he won't turn a deaf ear. He *will* respond.

The true personality of God the Father is not begrudging, but is rather what is shown at the end of this passage. He is generous and loving. He's not the kind to play pranks on us, to give us snakes or scorpions and then say, "Ha-ha.

Gotcha!" He wants the best for us and for our families. Verse 13 says he is even a better parent than we are, attending to our needs on multiple levels (giving the Spirit as well as daily bread).

So it is all right to present our needs to him . . . more than once. It is all right to plead with him regarding our children. Monica, the North African mother of centuries ago, bombarded heaven for fourteen years until her headstrong, lustful son finally yielded to Christ. His name: Augustine, eventual bishop of Hippo, the greatest Christian thinker of ancient times. He later wrote about "the mire of that deep pit, and the darkness of falsehood. . . . All which time that chaste, godly and sober widow . . . ceased not at all hours of her devotions to bewail my case unto You [God]."

Let us never be guilty of praying for our children *too little*. Let us ask, seek, knock. Persistence is not the same thing as impertinence. If we start to feel like a nag, we need only remember that the heavenly Son said it was OK.

While God will not run roughshod over our family members' wills, forcing them into his path whether they want to walk there or not, he is definitely on our side in *desiring* their surrender to him. That's good for a prayerful discussion anytime—even at midnight.

Lord, you don't mind if I get emotional
sometimes about my family needs, do you?
It's just that I want so strongly for my spouse
and children to follow you. I want the family
circle unbroken in heaven. Toward that end,

*use me to represent you well. And do what I
cannot do in wooing them to yourself.*

DOING THE WORD

Choose a time this week to spend thirty minutes praying exclusively for your family members. Spill out to God in detail what you wish for each of them. Believe that he has their very best interests at heart, and so begin looking for evidences of his response to your prayer.

WHAT HAPPENED, GOD?

One day Elisha went to Shunem. A prominent woman of the city invited him in to eat, and afterwards, whenever he passed that way, he stopped for dinner.

He talked to her as she stood in the doorway. "Next year at about this time you shall have a son!"

"O man of God," she exclaimed, "don't lie to me like that!"

But it was true; the woman soon conceived and had a baby boy the following year, just as Elisha had predicted.

One day when her child was older, he went out to visit his father, who was working with the reapers. He complained about a headache and soon was moaning in pain. His father said to one of the servants, "Carry him home to his mother."

So he took him home, and his mother held him on her lap; but around noontime he died. She carried him up to the bed of the prophet and shut the door; then she sent a

228

message to her husband: "Send one of the servants and a donkey so that I can hurry to the prophet and come right back."

"Why today?" he asked. "This isn't a religious holiday."

But she said, "It's important. I must go."

So she saddled the donkey and said to the servant, "Hurry! Don't slow down for my comfort unless I tell you to."

As she approached Mount Carmel, Elisha saw her in the distance and said to Gehazi, "Look, that woman from Shunem is coming. Run and meet her and ask her what the trouble is. See if her husband is all right and if the child is well."

"Yes," she told Gehazi, "everything is fine."

But when she came to Elisha at the mountain she fell to the ground before him and caught hold of his feet. Gehazi began to push her away, but the prophet said, "Let her alone; something is deeply troubling her and the Lord hasn't told me what it is."

Then she said, "It was you who said I'd have a son. And I begged you not to lie to me!"

Then he said to Gehazi, "Quick, take my staff! Don't talk to anyone along the way. Hurry! Lay the staff upon the child's face."

But the boy's mother said, "I swear to God that I won't go home without you." So Elisha returned with her.

Gehazi went on ahead and laid the staff upon the child's face, but nothing happened. There was no sign of life. He returned to meet Elisha and told him, "The child is still dead."

When Elisha arrived, the child was indeed dead, lying there upon the prophet's bed. He went in and shut the door behind him and prayed to the Lord. Then he lay upon the child's body, placing his mouth upon the child's mouth, and his eyes upon the child's eyes, and his hands upon the child's hands. And the child's body began to grow warm again! Then the prophet went down and walked back and forth in the house a few times; returning upstairs, he stretched himself again upon the child. This time the little boy sneezed seven times and opened his eyes!

Then the prophet summoned Gehazi. "Call her!" he said. And when she came in, he said, "Here's your son!" (2 Kings 4:8, 16-36)

He was his mother's pride and joy, the child she had never expected to bear, what with her husband already being elderly (v. 14). But the Lord had surprised her with a miracle baby, and so to her wealth and homestead was added a new little life, a son to carry on the family name, a burst of energy and delight.

Five, six, seven years went by—he was growing up so beautifully—and then came the awful morning in the field. This precious gift from heaven was suddenly struck with an aneurysm in the brain, or perhaps a seizure—screaming in agony, his eyes darting wildly from side to side, his cries echoing across the ravine. His father raced to cradle him in his arms. "What's wrong, Son?! Tell me what hurts." The boy could only press his palms against his temples before black-ing out. Servants rushed him out of the hot sun to the shelter of his mother's lap; she caressed his neck and pled for some faint flickering of the eyelids, but there was none. At noon, the shallow breathing stopped.

Where was God *now?* Had he not granted this child in the first place? How could he allow such subsequent cruelty?

Many a parent can testify to the fact that a miraculous conception, birth, or adoption is no guarantee of a smooth future. A storybook beginning can lurch drastically in the years that follow. That makes it hurt all the worse, because we expected great things from such an auspicious start. This child was to grow up to be a missionary, a Christian singer, a pastor—not a paraplegic, or a rebel, or a cultist.

For all who fear that the course of their child's life is suddenly derailing, the Shunammite woman offers a model. She wastes no time on hand-wringing and worry. She doesn't snarl at God. Instead, she immediately heads for his spokesman, brushing past intermediaries along the way. Neither her husband nor Gehazi can keep her from making contact with the divine power, the power that brought this child into being in the first place, the only power that can reverse the situation. Therein lies the *second* miracle.

When we think all is lost, when we wonder if God has played some kind of cruel joke on us, when all that we have worked so hard to implant in a child seems at risk—we must not give in to despair. "God who began the good work within you will keep right on helping you grow in his grace until his task within you is finally finished" (Phil. 1:6). It's always too soon to give up.

Lord, I am glad that you don't panic as easily
as I do. Reassure me today that you are still
in control of my family. Finish the plans
you have begun for each of us.

REINFORCING THE WORD

Turn to Philippians 1:6 in your Bible and underline it. In the margin write "2 Kings 4" to remind you of the story that illustrates this great truth about God's faithfulness in family crises.

Theater
of the Mind

"You have heard that it was said, 'Do not commit adultery.' But I tell you that anyone who looks at a woman lustfully has already committed adultery with her in his heart." (Matt. 5:27-28, NIV)

For though we live in the world, we do not wage war as the world does. The weapons we fight with are not the weapons of the world. On the contrary, they have divine power to demolish strongholds. We demolish arguments and every pretension that sets itself up against the knowledge of God, and we take captive every thought to make it obedient to Christ. (2 Cor. 10:3-5, NIV)

Why in the world did Jesus, the Author of grace and freedom, *tighten* the ban on extramarital sex? Wasn't the law of Moses tough enough when it said no fooling around? Then Jesus came along and said you couldn't even *think* about fooling around!

The Son of God was simply being realistic. He knew human nature well enough to know that men (and most women as well) don't *do* this kind of thing without *thinking* about it first. No one commits adultery without first mulling it over, contemplating, imagining what it would be like, even yearning for a liaison. The eye and the mind are busy long before the hotel door is closed.

So Jesus simply teaches that if you cut off illicit fantasies at the mental stage, you don't have to worry about the physical.

Paul calls for the same discipline when he says to "demolish . . . every pretension" (or pretend*ing*) and "take captive every thought to make it obedient." In other words, we say to our fertile imagination, "No. I will not allow that kind of *what-if*. I'm in charge here, and you will do what I say."

It is not wrong to be tempted. There will always be women or men more glamorous, more attractive, more visually exciting than the one you married (at least when you see them in public, at their best). If you're half-awake, you will no doubt notice their attributes. But it *is* wrong to let the temptation run on, to allow the thoughts to grow and expand and compound upon one another—instead of asserting your control.

Some notions are not to be tossed around—"on the one hand, on the other hand"—in a mental badminton game. They are rather to be stopped cold. A few years ago a popular singer crooned, "Oh, it's sad to belong to someone else when the right one comes along." Nonsense. The person to whom you belong as a result of marriage *is*, by definition, the right one. Case closed.

Tough-minded commitments and strong mental control are the best defenses against the heartbreak of infidelity.

———————————

Lord, I take up the weapon of your divine power to control my fantasies. Make me quick to tell myself no when I should. Help me not to linger over inappropriate scenes in the theater of the mind. Cause me rather to say, "All right, that's enough," and turn off the projector, knowing that you will bless me as I do.

DOING THE WORD

What one change could you make in your daily or weekly patterns that would help reduce the looking? It may be to avoid a certain newsstand, or alter your lunch arrangements, or shop in a different section of the video store. Choose one step, and do it.

ARE YOUR CHILDREN PROUD OF YOU?

> Parents are the pride of their children.
>
> (Prov. 17:6, NIV)

I sn't this backwards? Kids are supposed to make their *parents* proud of them. Children are to behave in such ways that they evoke that mushy line, "Oh, honey, you're just my pride and joy!"

This proverb proclaims the other side of what is apparently a two-way street. It says parents should give kids reason to be proud of *them.*

Are your children proud of you? Do they readily say to outsiders, "This is my dad" or "This is my mom"?

Granted, we adults have a tough time keeping up with our children's culture. We don't always know the latest vocabulary, clothing styles, or music artists. And as the teenage years come, a natural distancing takes place; teens want to be viewed as more independent.

But esteem is something deeper. It doesn't rest on what we

know about the young world. It rests on *who we are*—a person of integrity, of kindness, of fairness. A person who listens as well as lectures. A person who remembers how to laugh.

Dads can be bald, wear funny shirts, love '70s music—and still be appreciated for their deeper qualities. Moms can be oblivious to the latest teen styles and yet be esteemed as the one person a kid would run to in a crisis.

On the other hand, a father can look fine in public, but if he berates, belittles, ignores or—worst of all—abuses his off-spring behind closed doors, he will never be respected. Moms can look as attractive as the day they got married, but if they manipulate and harass, they will be shunned. Daughters and sons will stay as far away as they can.

In the life of the most healthy household, there will of course be times of tension and confrontation. But there will also be an abundance of camaraderie and joy, so that the younger generation can indeed admire the older, and aspire to be like them in years to come.

Lord, help me to set the kind of parenting
example that my kids can applaud today—
and imitate tomorrow.

DOING THE WORD

Think of someone you know whose children genuinely value them, don't mind being seen with them, and show that they're comfortable in their parents' presence. Study the interaction. What is it that makes the kids proud? If you can't seem to find clues, ask the parents directly, and see what you can learn.

STAYING POWER

"You must love the Lord your God and obey
every one of his commands. Listen! I am not talking now
to your children who have never experienced the Lord's
punishments or seen his greatness and his awesome
power. They weren't there to see the miracles he did in
Egypt against Pharaoh and all his land. They didn't see
what God did to the armies of Egypt and to their horses
and chariots—how he drowned them in the Red Sea as
they were chasing you, and how the Lord has kept them
powerless against you until this very day! They didn't
see how the Lord cared for you time and again through
all the years you were wandering in the wilderness, until your arrival here. They weren't there when Dathan
and Abiram (the sons of Eliab, descendants of Reuben)
sinned, and the earth opened up and swallowed them,
with their households and tents and all their belongings,
as all Israel watched!

"But *you* have seen these mighty miracles! How carefully, then, you should obey these commandments I am going to give you today, so that you may have the strength to go in and possess the land you are about to enter." (Deut. 11:1-8)

For every anguished Christian parent who watches his child veer away from the faith—for every godly mother or father who even *worries* about such a departure—this passage holds two important truths:

1. *Kids do not absorb God's ways by proxy.* The powerful events of our past, the red-letter days in our spiritual pilgrimage, carry no impact for them. We remember vividly the times we met God in a fresh way, the times he answered our prayer at a crucial moment, the times he corrected us. But to our children, these are merely bits of history. "They didn't see" (vv. 4-5); "they weren't there" (vv. 3, 6). Hence, they harbor no passion, only facts.

If the next generation is going to know the power, love, and justice of God, they will have to encounter him themselves.

2. *Even we adults have trouble at times retaining the lessons of the past—and we WERE there!* This is the point of Moses' plea to the Israelites just outside the Promised Land: *Beware of a short spiritual memory.* Don't let time dim your regard for the meaning of his miracles, his laws, his provisions, and his judgments.

It is good to ask ourselves occasionally, *What did God teach me five years ago? Ten? Twenty? What kernels of insight did I gain back at wedding time, at the birth of my first child, or during a crisis encounter with God?*

Have we ever exclaimed, "I'll never forget this moment—

I'll remember this as long as I live"? The Israelites said the same thing. Yet they swerved into idolatry within decades of the death of Joshua, Moses' successor. We too will fade away from our sense of God's power and God's standards unless we consciously keep them alive in our hearts.

There's no such thing as a spiritual gene that silently passes, like blond hair or math aptitude, from one generation to the next. Each person must build his or her own altar, invite the fire of God to fall, and then keep blowing on the coals.

Lord, I thank you for all you've invested
in me thus far. I want to keep my spiritual
flame burning brightly, to the very end of my
days. Ignite my children as well. Give them
their own Red Sea experiences to remember
and cherish. Because without you
we will only grow cold and gray.

REINFORCING THE WORD

Plan a trip—a pilgrimage, if you will—back to the location of a previous high point in your spiritual life: the house, camp, or church where you first committed your life to Christ, the place where you sought God in desperate prayer and he answered, the spot where you first stepped out in some form of ministry or service. This may be just a few miles away, or it may have to be worked into next summer's vacation plans in another state or province. Use the pilgrimage to help you and your family remember God's goodness in your life.

Every Parent's Dream

Unless the Lord builds a house, the builders' work is useless. Unless the Lord protects a city, sentries do no good. It is senseless for you to work so hard from early morning until late at night, fearing you will starve to death; for God wants his loved ones to get their proper rest.

Children are a gift from God; they are his reward. Children born to a young man are like sharp arrows to defend him.

Happy is the man who has his quiver full of them. That man shall have the help he needs when arguing with his enemies. (Ps. 127)

Blessings on all who reverence and trust the Lord—on all who obey him!

Their reward shall be prosperity and happiness. Your wife shall be contented in your home. And look at all those children! There they sit around the dinner table as vigorous and healthy as young olive trees. That is God's reward to those who reverence and trust him.

May the Lord continually bless you with heaven's blessings as well as with human joys. May you live to enjoy your grandchildren! And may God bless Israel! (Ps. 128)

H ere's everything you've ever wanted as a parent. These two short psalms fairly overflow with delicious images:

- a good night's sleep (127:2)
- children who actually seem like a gift (127:3)
- children who stick up for you in public! (127:4-5)
- a contented spouse (128:3)
- good-looking kids around the dinner table (128:3)
- living long enough to enjoy your grandchildren (128:6)

What more could any parent want?

Such bliss is not just a happy accident; it comes from specific causes. A successful home life begins with admitting that you and I cannot create it alone; the Lord must build the house (127:1). While there is much we can do, we cannot do it all. If God is not invited to work in our households, to protect us from danger or stupidity, to make this odd collection of headstrong individuals work together smoothly, we will spend our years in frustration.

The rewards of Psalm 128 rain down upon a certain kind of parent: those "who reverence and trust the Lord." It says so twice, in verses 1 and 4. Our common sense is not enough. Pop psychology and self-help books won't do the trick.

Parenting, as philosopher Michael Novak once wrote in a *Harper's* magazine essay, "brings breathtaking vistas of our inadequacy." That is, he added, because "to have children is, plainly, to cease being a child oneself."

But when we cast our shortcomings upon the Lord and admit that we aren't entirely mature ourselves, that we still need to finish growing up even as we guide young ones in doing the same, he has a way of making things gel after all. Our dreams for family life start to become reality, because he has been given freedom to work.

———————

Lord, I dearly want a family that succeeds, that smiles, that loves each other, that brings out the best in all of us. And I know I can't do it alone. I need you. Take charge; make good things happen under our roof. I trust you to build this house as only you can.

REFLECTING ON THE WORD

Write out five heartfelt wishes regarding your family. What five things would make you feel *terrific* about your home life? Then discuss your list with the Lord, sorting out what you can do to bring about your dreams and what only he can do.

APPENDIXES

THE "HELP!" INDEX

H ere are some of the best Scriptures to read when facing particular marriage and parenting stresses.

When you've lost your temper
Ephesians 4:26-27
James 1:19-20
(See "'You Make Me So Mad!'" p. 100)

When you're waiting for someone to come home
Psalm 91

When your child won't obey
Proverbs 29:15-17
(See "Boundaries Are Not Bad," p. 48)

When you have to move
Deuteronomy 31:3-8

When you're pregnant
Luke 1:39-55
Psalm 127
(See "Every Parent's Dream," p. 242)

When you wish you were pregnant
1 Samuel 1:2-20
(See "When No One Understands," p. 176)

When your pregnancy isn't going well
Genesis 25:21-23
Psalm 31

When you're "too old" to be pregnant!
Luke 1
(See "Living with God's Surprises," pp. 153–162)

When the money isn't stretching far enough
Psalm 37:16-26
(See "Paying the Bills," p. 216)
2 Kings 4:1-7
(See "Crunch Time for a Single Mom," p. 25)

When your spouse didn't support you in front of the children or friends
2 Timothy 4:16-18

When you've just had an argument
Romans 12:15-21
(See "The Fine Art of Peacemaking," p. 79)

When a family member is ill
Mark 1:29-31
James 5:13-18
(See "When Sickness Strikes," p. 73)
Luke 8:41-56
(See "Never Too Rushed," p. 54)

SPECIAL SCRIPTURES FOR SINGLE MOTHERS

Genesis 21:8-21
(See "Innocent Victim," p. 97)

2 Kings 4:1-7
(See "Crunch Time for a Single Mom," p. 25)

Psalm 10:12-18

Psalm 27

Psalm 121

Proverbs 15

Isaiah 30:18-26

Isaiah 54:4-8

Romans 8:18-39

1 Corinthians 10:12-13;
Hebrews 4:14-16

Galatians 6:7-10
(See "Tired?" p. 22)

Philippians 4:5-20

1 Timothy 5:3-16

Hebrews 6:10-12

1 Peter 1

SPECIAL SCRIPTURES FOR SINGLE FATHERS

Genesis 19:23-38
(a stern warning from
the life of Lot)

Genesis 37, 42–49
(Jacob's later years)

1 Samuel 2:12-34; 3:11-13
*(See "No, You Don't,"
p. 183)*

Psalm 27

Psalm 103:8-18
*(See "The Soft Side of
Fathering," p. 103)*

Psalm 121

Proverbs 15

Isaiah 30:18-26

Romans 8:18-39

1 Corinthians 10:12-13;
   Hebrews 4:14-16

Galatians 6:7-10
   (See "Tired?" p. 22)

Philippians 4:5-20

Hebrews 6:10-12

1 Peter 1

150 BEST SCRIPTURES FOR YOUR CHILD TO MEMORIZE

M ost Christian parents have a love/hate relationship with Bible memorization. They think it's a marvelous goal. If their child could recite ten Scriptures from memory, they'd be so proud. And the verses would surely be an anchor for their son or daughter in tough times to come . . . the teenage years, going away to college. Verses are like vitamins and vegetables; every youngster *ought* to be ingesting a regular dose.

But *how?* In our helter-skelter households, who has time to make this happen? And won't kids just forget the verses anyway? It may have worked back in the placid 1950s, but things are different today. . . . Such logic soothes our consciences for a while, until guilt comes again to the surface.

None of this, however, dents the truth of Psalm 119:9-11 (NIV):

How can a young man keep his way pure?
   By living according to your word.
I seek you with all my heart;

> Do not let me stray from your commands.
> I have hidden your word in my heart
> That I might not sin against you.

God's Word in the heart and brain is a strategic hedge against sin.

And it is simply a neurological fact that the easiest memorizing happens between the ages of four and twelve. The average grade-schooler's mind can stash away prodigious amounts of Scripture (or song lyrics, or baseball batting averages, or baton troupe routines). The young cerebrum is a vast maze of invisible grooves, just waiting for data. What kind of data will it be?

There's another neurological fact, however, that must be stated: *Memorization without review is pointless.* Zero. A waste of time.

Shouldn't that be obvious? Stop a minute and try to recite your telephone number from two or three towns ago. You used to know it perfectly. Why can't you come up with it now?

Because you haven't had any recent review.

Thus, memorizing a Bible verse is the easy part. Retaining it requires a system of review. Here's a system that has worked well in our family for two generations:

Somewhere around the time I turned four years old, my parents began writing on three-by-five cards the verses I memorized in Sunday school as well as at their initiative. The verse was written on one side, the reference on the other, and the cards were kept in a recipe box. As soon as I learned to write, I was allowed to do my own copying from the Bible.

(These specimens of early handwriting are now a source of delightful comment from my family!)

One or more times a week, my mother would sit down and listen to ten to fifteen minutes of recitation, one card after another. Sometimes this happened after a meal, other times in the car. A stiff cardboard place-marker moved through the deck, from Genesis to Revelation and back again. It was a great parent-child activity, and in this way, the verses memorized were retained.

The result? Today, more than three decades later, the vast majority of those six-hundred-plus verses have "stuck."

My wife and I did the same with our children, building their files week by week. We opted for a modern translation of Scripture, so they could grasp the fullest possible meaning. And again we found that the more frequent the review, the more pleasant the experience, because the child didn't have to struggle. If we went too long between recitations, their memories became rusty, and the whole process became drudgery. In other words, use it or lose it.

The most fun times, of course, were when the kids would haul out Dad's box from childhood. They wanted to see if the old man still knew his Scripture.

The great truths of the Bible do no good lying ink-bound in a closed book. If we mean for the next generation to live godly lives, we must take time to implant God's parameters from the beginning, making the process as creative and stimulating as possible.

Here is a recommended list of Scriptures to memorize, starting from the easiest for young children (both in vocabulary and meaning) and proceeding to the more complex.

1 John 4:19	John 3:16-17
Psalm 23:1	1 John 4:4
Psalm 4:8 (for bedtimes)	James 1:19
Psalm 46:1	2 Timothy 1:7
Genesis 1:1	John 10:11
Hebrews 13:8	Psalm 19:14
Exodus 20:12	Matthew 6:33
Colossians 3:23	1 Thessalonians 4:11
Psalm 51:10	Romans 5:8
Psalm 118:24	Colossians 4:6
1 Peter 5:7	Psalm 37:4-5
Matthew 22:37-39	Luke 21:33
1 Timothy 4:12	Revelation 3:20
Psalm 119:11	2 Timothy 2:15
John 14:6	Luke 18:16
Psalm 119:105	Romans 6:23
Luke 2:52	Acts 24:16
1 John 1:8-9	James 1:22
Proverbs 20:11	Psalm 37:23-25
Habakkuk 2:20	Mark 8:36-37
Romans 2:11	Psalm 66:18
John 1:1-3	John 8:32, 36
Proverbs 18:24	Psalm 107:8-9
1 Thessalonians 5:18	Romans 10:9-10
Romans 3:23	Proverbs 15:1

Acts 1:8

1 John 5:14-15

Psalm 141:3

James 4:7

Deuteronomy 31:8

Luke 19:10

2 Thessalonians 3:3

Psalm 139:23-24

Romans 8:28

1 John 2:15-17

Hebrews 13:17

1 Samuel 3:19

John 14:27

2 Timothy 2:3-4

1 Samuel 16:7

Luke 12:48

Matthew 16:26

Romans 14:12

John 6:37

1 Peter 3:12

Proverbs 14:12

Micah 6:8

John 3:30

1 Samuel 18:14

Romans 1:16

Matthew 11:28-30

Isaiah 26:3

Luke 21:34

Jeremiah 29:11-13

Romans 8:38-39

1 Corinthians 4:2

Matthew 28:18-20

Proverbs 3:5-7

1 Timothy 6:6-12

John 1:11-14

1 Kings 18:21

James 5:15-16

Ephesians 4:26-32

Luke 9:23

1 Peter 3:15

2 Timothy 2:22-24

Proverbs 27:1-2

Philippians 1:6

Romans 12:1-2

Acts 4:12

Philippians 4:13

Proverbs 10:5

Galatians 5:22-23

1 Corinthians 6:19-20

Daniel 1:8

Matthew 7:13-14
Hebrews 4:16
1 Thessalonians 4:16-18
Romans 12:10
Proverbs 10:23

John 4:24
Daniel 3:17-18
Ephesians 5:18
Ecclesiastes 5:10
1 Corinthians 10:13

Jonah 2:7
Hebrews 11:6
Matthew 6:24
Philippians 4:8
2 Corinthians 5:17

Lamentations 3:27-28
Isaiah 53:5-6
Philippians 4:19
Matthew 6:34
Titus 2:6-8

Hebrews 12:11
Galatians 6:7-10
Philippians 1:29
2 Chronicles 7:14
Isaiah 40:31

Isaiah 41:10
Matthew 6:19-21
2 Corinthians 4:17-18
Isaiah 6:8
Ephesians 2:8-9

Psalm 34:18-19
Matthew 5:3-16 (the Beatitudes)
Malachi 3:10
Joshua 1:8-9
Isaiah 1:18-19

Esther 4:14
Isaiah 48:18
Rest of Psalm 23
Isaiah 55:6-11
Psalm 1

Philippians 2:3-16
1 Chronicles 28:9
Numbers 23:19
Deuteronomy 30:19
Amos 5:23-24

Deuteronomy 6:6-9
Psalm 91
1 Corinthians 13
Luke 2:7-16 (Christmas story)
And finally: 2 Timothy 3:15-17

SPIRITUAL HIGHLIGHTS OF OUR FAMILY

WHAT OUR WEDDING MEANT TO US SPIRITUALLY

_____

_____

_____

_____

_____

_____

A SPECIAL TIME WHEN WE COMMITTED OUR MARRIAGE TO GOD

_____

_____

_____

_____

_____

_____

_____

OUR CHILDREN'S
DEDICATIONS/CHRISTENINGS/BAPTISMS

OUR CHILDREN'S COMMITMENTS
TO FOLLOW CHRIST

_____

_____

_____

_____

_____

_____

_____

OTHER SPIRITUAL TURNING
POINTS IN OUR FAMILY

_____

_____

_____

_____

_____

_____

_____

REMARKABLE ANSWERS TO PRAYER IN OUR FAMILY

_____

_____

_____

_____

_____

_____

_____

_____

_____

_____

_____

_____

_____

_____

_____

_____